T3-BSD-740

DORIS LESSING: THE ALCHEMY OF SURVIVAL

DORIS LESSING: THE ALCHEMY OF SURVIVAL

EDITED BY

Carey Kaplan and
Ellen Cronan Rose

Ohio University Press books are printed on acid-free paper.

Library of Congress Cataloging-in-Publication Data

Doris Lessing : the alchemy of survival.

Includes bibliographies.
1. Lessing, Doris May, 1919- —Criticism and intrepretation. I. Kaplan, Carey. II. Rose, Ellen Cronan, 1938-
PR6023.E833Z62 1988 823′.914 87-34777
ISBN 0-8214-0891-7

Contents

Introduction

Selected Essays

INTRODUCTION

CAREY KAPLAN AND
ELLEN CRONAN ROSE

1. Lessing and Her Readers: Celebrating Difference

On April 25, 1984, Doris Lessing appeared on the popular nightly news program, National Public Radio's "All Things Considered," where interviewer Susan Stamberg pressed her to account for her move from traditional realist fiction to the "space fiction" of *Briefing for a Descent into Hell* and the *Canopus in Argos* series. "About your shift from realistic writing to fantasy writing or visionary writing," Stamberg asked, "do you have some sense of what the role of the writer should be? . . . Is it to show us the world as it is, or the world as it should be, or the world as it might be?" "Why do you make it 'or, or, or?' " Lessing retorted. "It could be 'and, and, and.' " Later she returned to this point, suggesting that "either/or" has "very little to do with how things really are . . . Because you know that's how the computer works. They call it the binary mode, don't they? The *this* or *that*, the switch. This or that. I'm asking myself, is the computer, the way it functions, a model of the human mind?"[1]

The fiction of Doris Lessing, which rejects simple binary opposites and insists on a construction of reality that rejects nothing, limits nothing, and includes everything by saying "and, and, and," rather than "either/or," exemplifies *differance* which Jacques Derrida insists is "neither a *word* nor a *concept*"[2] but includes three significations, all of which help explain the variety and richness of Lessing's writing: (1) "to differ"—to be unlike or dissimilar in nature; (2) "to defer"—to delay, postpone; and (3) "diferre" (Latin)—to scatter, disperse. Lessing's works embody all three of these significations and hence defy the pigeonholing dear to the hearts of academics. The essence of Lessing's philosophical pursuit of the big questions about the meaning of life, truth, and reality is the acknowledgment of simple difference: that people, cultures, events, places, and times are all unlike and separate, irreconcilable, even if they are, on the other hand and at the same time, part of a vast whole scattered about the universe, the meaning of which must be deferred until our feeble human brains attain some new level of evolution. Additionally, what the Sufis call the "scatter technique"[3] underlies much of Lessing's writing—concepts, ideas, and themes are fragmented and dispersed throughout each book and throughout the body of her work, recurring metamorphosed in new books, requiring adaptations of understanding on the part of readers. Because an image or a theme may recur at any time, transformed and reworked, the work resists final analysis. For example, at the beginning of *Martha Quest*, the first book in the *Children of Violence* series, Martha has a vision of the ideal city, geometrical, hierarchical, multiracial, full of gardens and gentle people. In the context of *Martha Quest* and subsequent books, that vision has significance and weight both in Martha's life and in the world of the whole *Children of Violence* series. But it is not until *The Four-Gated City* that Martha's original vision attains a comprehensive and ironic resonance, thus recreating the meaning of the first four books of the series in its light. The reader is asked to balance the vision of the city against the reality of war-gutted London and against Mark's dismal city of refugees. With this final reworking of the theme, the exhausted critic may sit back and sigh, "Well, at least I've pegged *that* motif." No such luck. For the city continues to recur confusingly and disturbingly as an implicit irony in books like *Briefing for a Descent into Hell* and *Memoirs of a Survivor*. And perhaps, but not certainly finally, the city looms once more in Lessing's *Canopus* novels, geometrical, charmed, magnetic, magical, doomed—the image folding in on itself and expanding like some organic, respirating creature. Such scattered meaning, such rejection of definition, such *differance*, demands delay and postponement.

Lessing's work can be viewed as a whole or as a series of

interrelated wholes (*Children of Violence*; the *Canopus in Argos: Archives* books; the stories; the Jane Somers diaries). It is still in the process of becoming, still full of surprises, play, audacity, dogma, recantation, and grouchy dismissal of critical appraisal. The critic cannot even pin down Lessing's identity, which shifts within the person Doris Lessing from self-declared hard-core realist to self-declared, equally hard-core fantasist; from Communist to student of R.D. Laing to student of Sufism; from a "small, personal voice" to the spokesperson of the cosmos; from adolescent girl to aging woman. Nor can the critic be sure that Doris Lessing is Doris Lessing. Recently she fractured into Jane Somers. And what of *Retreat to Innocence* which Lessing has disowned but which ineluctably exists? Within individual books, identity shifts mystifyingly, most notably in *The Golden Notebook* in which Doris Lessing writes about Anna Wulf who writes about Anna Wulf who writes about Ella who writes about a nameless suicidal young man.

Clearly (or perhaps obscurely) meaning in the works of Lessing never sits still. Because Lessing refuses certainty, the critic too treads quicksand.

Lessing is an alchemical writer. More than any other major twentieth-century writer—excepting, possibly, D.H. Lawrence—Lessing challenges her readers and changes them; alters their consciousnesses; radicalizes their sexual, personal, and global politics. She writes, as John Carey noted in the early sixties, about certain themes specific to late-twentieth-century consciousness: "Race; the conflict of the generations; the man-woman relationship; the problems of the creative artist; and politics."[4] But underneath these undeniably vital concerns is an even more profound and utterly relentless investigation of the nature of reality. What is reality? What is freedom? What is truth? What is the meaning of life? Lessing's self-imposed task has been on the massive philosophical scale of writers like George Eliot, Tolstoy or Proust, all of whom have prominent places in her literary pantheon. Lessing, however, is different and special in that she alone has explored philosophical questions through the medium of female experience. In Lessing's books, women and women's experience are seen as important enough to pose the big questions. In her work, questions and suggestions about the meaning of life and the nature of reality do not emerge from the ultimate challenge of war and perilous adventure, which, for example in *The Golden Notebook*, are pushed to the background, but from such seemingly prosaic events and experiences as a first dance, marriage, pregnancy, menstruation, female sexuality, romantic love, housekeeping, childrearing, and friendship between women. As author Lisa Alther (*Kinflicks*, *Original Sins*, *Other Women*) remarks, "I could never have started writing novels without having read Doris Lessing's books. I learned from her, to my enormous surprise, that a novel could be serious and philosophical even if the protagonist were an ordinary woman, neither a whore nor a goddess, and even if the content were nothing more ambitious than the stuff of daily life. Lessing's books were a revelation."[5]

Lessing's books are striking, too, and demand fresh critical approaches because in them women prevail and have futures. Lessing, more than any other writer, has freed women from the literally dead endings usually available for female protagonists through the beginning of the twentieth century: suicide, death, madness, marriage (and a vague, unspecified happily-ever-after). Lessing mocks this tradition and reconstitutes it. The novel-within-a-novel "Free Women," which is the frame for the notebooks of *The Golden Notebook*, self-consciously subverts the conventional ending. We the readers know that "Free Women" is the novel Anna Wulf writes after she has experienced everything she describes in the larger novel. We feel fairly confident that her life goes on, rich, complicated, unconventional. Yet Anna's novel, "Free Women," about an even more fictional Anna Wulf than Doris Lessing's Anna, the protagonist of *The Golden Notebook*, ends with Molly marrying and Anna getting a job as a marriage counselor. This is all a joke, satirizing the ending appropriate to women's novels. Lessing refuses the necessity and opens new possibilities.

We don't know what becomes of Anna. All we know is that she writes a novel, "Free Women," as a result of her mad affair with Saul. After that? Anything we can imagine: work, family, friends, love, sex, politics, the rich melange of late-twentieth-century London literary and left-political life. Nothing restrictive. Her life heretofore has been as experimental and provisional as her story told in bits and pieces in *The Golden Notebook.* Why should Anna dwindle into anything less than the protean creature we have followed so tortuously through hundreds of pages? One of Lessing's reiterated points in *The Golden Notebook* is that the artist is of necessity beyond the work she is able to produce, already looking back in order to create. Anna, too, we can safely assume, has moved on beyond the limitations of "Free Women." Whatever else she may be, she is surely not a marriage counselor.

A related facet of Lessing's writing that has befuddled critics and demanded an original critical endeavor is her disinterest in style. Much of the fascination of the modernist and postmodernist canon has been stylistic; to some extent, style has come to define excellence. Brilliant verbal pyrotechnics dazzle readers of twentieth-century writers from Joyce to Pynchon, requiring analysis, elucidation, and even careful translation. Lessing, however, although she is certainly interested in structure, particularly in *The Golden Notebook*, rarely indulges in wordplay, *double entendre*, trope, motif, symbol, mythology, in all the playfulness that characterizes much of the most highly regarded literature of the past fifty years. If we consider the wordplay of writers like Nabokov a reification of language, a rather extreme expression of a "masculine" tendency to objectify and seek abstraction,[6] then Lessing's writing may be usefully described as "feminine"— material, solid, and concrete.

Lessing is all passionate engagement; she repudiates again and again the distancing implicit in the chilly cerebral detachment of highly wrought style. Indeed, Lessing's stylistic strategy has worked resolutely in a different direction. Her novels are often presented as diaries, memoirs, personal archival records, letters, notebooks, and rough drafts. Her material is notoriously autobiographical, so that the line between writer and subject is blurred and mystifying. Even when Lessing treats intellectual notions, political ideology, and cosmic teleology, her tone is passionate, deeply personal, emotional, and even physical. Long before the women's movement enunciated the dictum, "the personal is political," Lessing's books demonstrated the point repeatedly and forcefully. In *Children of Violence*, for instance, Martha comes to understand the enormity of genocide through her intense physical connection with Thomas Stern; she recognizes the oppression of women by men and by biology during the course of her pregnancy; she becomes a Communist because of her longing for community, her need to obliterate her excoriating sense of isolation; she comprehends the Collective Unconscious through her identification with Lynda's madness; she experiences the fragmentation of late-twentieth-century society by raising a house full of children, each of whom is differently affected by the various accidents of recent history; she expresses her political and social consciousness at any given time by how she dresses and does her hair and by how much she weighs.

Lessing's subject matter and style thus demand a new and different kind of criticism because her writing is as original, feminine, immediate, and raw as the diaries she frequently imitates. Lessing's resistance to the dominant literary mode may help account, we suspect, for her slow acceptance as a major literary figure. John Carey underscores this slow acceptance when he describes his efforts to publish his 1965 dissertation on Lessing: "However when the manuscript was submitted, after a lengthy delay I eventually received a rejection. The rejection was based on a single reader who had no major fault to find with my work, but felt that Lessing was not a major modern figure and did not deserve a serious scholarly book devoted to her."[7] Frederick P.W. McDowell, attempting to publish an article on Lessing's achievement to date in 1965, encountered the same problem: "Some editors confessed ignorance of her, and others thought she was not important enough."[8]

Perhaps these early readers of Lessing criticism were unable to appreciate her importance because their expectations about "serious" literature were so confiningly modernist. Looking for wit and wordplay, they found instead a surface of unselfconscious fiction written in a dated nineteenth-century realist mode. Their expectations flouted, they were perhaps prevented from seeing beneath the apparently traditional surface to the unconventional and even revolutionary content and structure. Hence, the slow recognition of Lessing was left not to the critical establishment but to scattered sympathetic individuals, to "common readers," some of whom happened to be academics. Those first readers who were also academics longed to engage in critical discourse about this new writer whose content was original, even unprecedented, but who they knew was not strictly an academic commodity, given current critical standards. When these academics came together, in their gratitude for one another and for Lessing's *differance*, they engendered atypically generous, eclectic, and innovative criticism and pedagogy.

From the beginnings of Lessing scholarship in the United States, readers approached Lessing's books for reasons other than her possible academic viability. John Carey, for example, who wrote the first American doctoral dissertation on Lessing in 1965, looks back on his reasons for working on an author relatively unknown in the United States in the early sixties. He concludes: "*The Golden Notebook* had a profound effect on my life and influenced me in a number of personal ways."[9]

Responsive readers and academics in the early sixties recognized, with a rush of enthusiasm, that new and necessary forms and consciousness were suddenly available in literature. Their lives were being named and described in ways they had vaguely and incoherently longed for and vainly sought. For many people, women and men, reading Lessing's books aroused a burgeoning excitement which they needed to share with like-minded colleagues.

"Cooperation," "a noncompetitive community of scholars," "singular lack of territoriality"—such phrases and words continually recur when early appreciators of Doris Lessing recall the formation of the Doris Lessing Society and the *Doris Lessing Newsletter*. As Dee Seligman announced in the founding issue of the *Newsletter*, "The purpose of the *Doris Lessing Newsletter* is to facilitate the sharing of ideas and information among serious readers of Doris Lessing. In six years of seminars on Lessing at the Modern Language Association's annual meeting, I have seen a spirit of co-operation and interest in one another's research and ideas which is different both quantitatively and qualitatively from similar seminars presented at the meeting."[10]

From the early sixties on, an authentic community of scholars formed to discuss and exchange perceptions about a compelling writer of extraordinary power and range who left her mark not only on thinking but also on lives. Seligman, in explaining the founding of the *Newsletter*, describes her initial sense of this unusual group of academics: "It was a time of great excitement and new experience for me, and coincidentally, the time of my first pregnancy. I found myself part of a rapidly growing network of Lessing readers. People started to write to me from other parts of the country and foreign countries as well. . . . My awareness of the size of the Lessing readership stretched further than I had ever understood, and I began to feel that I might help to make more of these connections happen."[11] The language of this memoir is entirely typical of Lessing scholarship in its unconventional tone—personal, direct, using Carol Gilligan's vocabulary of female intimacy ("network," "connection"), and even mentioning a vital and archetypal female experience as somehow related to the critical endeavor. This is not to say that Lessing scholarship has not been serious, rigorous, and thoroughly professional—for it has been and is all of these things. But it is to say that the academic critical response to Lessing has had dimensions absent from critical response to other important contemporary writers. The deeply personal involvement of readers in Lessing's books has created a body of comment and analysis that is broad in scope, multifaceted in approach, cooperative in nature, and continually evolving. As Seligman emphasizes, Lessing enthusiasts have flourished everywhere, and they have longed to share their varying and various interpretations and notions. In fact, the progress of Lessing's increasing reputation is unusual for a major literary figure. Lessing's reputation has not been the work of a critical school, of a coterie, or of a well-known promoter. Her books touched people and they in turn reached out to others similarly affected, yearning to discuss their perceptions.

Paul Schlueter, for example, whose organizational efforts

were instrumental in founding the Doris Lessing Society, is typical of the many scholars who engaged with Lessing's books for unorthodox reasons. Schlueter was assigned *The Golden Notebook* in a graduate course, but what convinced him of the book's status was its powerful applicability to his own life: "I was amazed at how much it spoke to me and my own situation, nearing the pressure point . . . in my first marriage."[12] Schlueter, who published the second book on Lessing (the late Dorothy Brewster's 1965 Twayne volume was the first), convened the first MLA panel on her work in 1971, signing up thirty-five academics, the maximum number permitted, but actually chairing a lively discussion among forty or more enthusiasts.

The history of the *Doris Lessing Newsletter* demonstrates the informal but often impassioned and unconventional communication between early Lessing scholars that went on in the interim between, and behind the scenes of, annual meetings of the MLA. From its first issue in 1976, the *Newsletter* was designed as a forum for the exchange of ideas, notes, teaching hints. Unfinished and preliminary articles were encouraged. This design fostered an intimate, cooperative spirit as well as a reading of Lessing that was provisional and ongoing rather than frozen and officially academic. In the pages of the *Newsletter* it is possible to see critics pursuing a scholarly interest which was also an active engagement, directly influencing their lives. In volume 2, number 2, for instance, Lois Marchino begins her piece, "Life, Lessing and the Pursuit of Feminist Criticism," by asking a series of questions: "How can we respond to the challenges Lessing puts before us as critics? How could we be Lessing readers—especially all of us women who are teaching in universities—without worrying about the question, and not only about our criticism, but about our participation in the institutions, about our lives? What kind of criticism can we write, especially since Lessing covers everything herself?" (p. 1). Marchino goes on to say that she is writing this article "because I like to think and talk about Lessing—it's such a good platform for springing into oneself and beyond." Here, then, are all the elements that typify and distinguish the critics addressing themselves to Lessing: the sense of personal as well as literary engagement; the application of Lessing's novels and stories about Rhodesia and England to U.S. academic life; the sense of ongoing discourse; and the awareness of alchemy, the awareness that investigation of Lessing's works will lead to inner and outer change. In early issues of the *Newsletter*, Dee Seligman ran a "Help Needed" note which read in part, "In this age of tremendous pressure to publish or perish, college and university faculty seek status-granting publications for their ideas. However, the purpose of this *Newsletter* is to beat the system and to allow scholars to talk and share with one another, rather than to publish long critical articles which a very small number are interested in. Lessing readers have often been changed by what they have read, or certainly they are moved to see their lives in a different perspective. My own experience is that her readers want to share with one another that effect which Lessing has had on them and on their students" (*Newsletter* 2, no. 2 [Winter 1978]: 3).

In 1980 the *Newsletter* moved from Dee Seligman's personal aegis to Old Dominion University and the joint editorship of Paul Schlueter and Nancy Topping Bazin. From this time on, the *Newsletter's* tone is at once more scholarly and less conversational. But the intense and sincere exchange of ideas continued with, for example, Roberta Rubenstein's long response to reviews by Paul Schlueter and Judith Stitzel of her book, *The Novelistic Vision of Doris Lessing: Breaking the Forms of Consciousness*. Rubenstein begins her response by saying, "In the laudable tradition of the *Doris Lessing Newsletter*, I would like to continue the dialogue on Lessing scholarship by responding to the reviews of my book" (4, no. 1 [Summer 1980]: 9).

In the next issue, Claire Sprague, first president of the newly formed Doris Lessing Society, described the goals of the organization, emphasizing the special nature of Lessing studies: "The Doris Lessing Seminars, going back to 1971, and the *Newsletter*, started in 1976, helped to create a history and an attitude of cooperation that the Society has inherited. I know I am one of many who have been helped by that history and that attitude" (4, no. 2 [Winter 1980]: 2).

Under the editorship of Sprague, the *Newsletter* has extended its "laudable tradition" geographically, with guest editors from Britain and South Africa. And the Doris Lessing Society now includes among its members scholars from Germany, Great Britain, Japan, South Africa, and the Scandinavian countries. But internationalization has merely enhanced dialogue, as foreign scholars bring new theoretical and ideological perspectives, in addition to foreign accents, to panels the society regularly mounts, as an Allied Organization, at the MLA's annual convention.

In addition to the cooperation that distinguishes Lessing criticism, its other remarkable quality is its complex eclecticism, arising from this widespread readership. No single scholar has said, or, indeed, tried to say, the definitive word on Lessing. Instead, recognizing that one of Lessing's dominant and most poignant themes is the impossibility of absolute definition, the fragmentary nature of reality, the modern world's resistance to assignment of meaning, academics have tacitly engaged in a critical endeavor that is always seeking, never static. Because Lessing's books never allow the reader to settle down comfortably, respectful scholars, learning life stances as well as literature from Lessing, have also never settled but have approached the books and stories from all available critical directions: Jungian/archetypal; Marxist; Freudian; reader response; feminist; New Critical; semiotic and deconstructionist—and combinations of several of these. None have contained Lessing's work but all have elucidated it.

The eleven essays we have assembled represent both the diversity of approaches scholars have taken to Lessing's *oeuvre* since 1971, when they began meeting to share their views at the annual MLA convention, and the creative *differance* of their colloquy. Frederick C. Stern's own bracketed comments, written in 1986 about his 1973 essay, constitute an extreme and dramatic example of the dialectical progress of Lessing criticism as well as of Marxist methodology. And the differences *within* Marxist criticism of Lessing are well represented in the essays that follow. To understand the changing form of Lessing's novels, Stern uses the Lukacsian notion of *Weltanschauung*, while

Alvin Sullivan invokes Pierre Macherey's concept of the "decentered" text and Molly Hite, who like Sullivan concentrates on the "gaps and cracks" through which Lessing reveals (and subverts) the "ideology" of coherence, uses an essentially Marxist theoretical framework unself-consciously. Katherine Fishburn situates her pedagogy in the Marxist-feminist tradition of Lillian Robinson, and Eve Bertelsen's discussion of the ideological function served by editing literary interviews relies on Louis Althusser.

Reading the essays in sequence, you will often see collegial dialogue enacted. Frederick Stern strikes the keynote to which one essayist after another will return, in observing that Lessing is "an intensely political writer." He argues, however, that despite her much-publicized membership in the Communist party, "Lessing's commitment from the beginning of her work . . . was not to Marxist thought and its revolutionary components but rather to radical humanist thought." Molly Hite builds, as it were, on this assumption to observe that *The Golden Notebook* constitutes a "critique of Marxist ideology." But her analysis of that novel and of *The Four-Gated City* calls into question Stern's assertion that Lessing is a "radical humanist." For the ideological base of humanism is a belief in the transcendent self, a belief undercut by these texts' radical skepticism about the unity and coherence of character.

Hite characterizes Lessing's 1957 essay, "The Small Personal Voice," as a nostalgic paean to a humanism she would subsequently repudiate, but Jeanne Murray Walker finds in that early essay the structuring dialectic that shapes Lessing's 1975 "attempt at autobiography," *The Memoirs of a Survivor*. In "The Small Personal Voice," Lessing says that the writer's task is to portray "the responsible individual voluntarily submitting his will to the collective, but never finally; and insisting on making his own personal and private judgements before every act of submission" (p. 12). *Memoirs*, Walker demonstrates convincingly, insists that our survival as a race depends on a "reciprocity" between both the "different aspects of one personality" and "among individuals" who comprise the collective, "society."

Walker emphasizes both the necessity for and the problems of "social exchange" between individuals in society. Elizabeth Abel specifies the "problem" of exchange in feminist terms. Drawing on Levi-Strauss's *Elementary Structures of Kinship*, she argues that patriarchy depends on a "cycle of reciprocity" established when men "exchange" women in an exogamous kinship system. Lessing's portrayal of brother-sister incest, in *The Golden Notebook* and in the short story "Each Other," offers a radical challenge to patriarchal politics, Abel asserts. "Allegiance to the brother can insulate women from a political and sexual hierarchy determined by men."

If Marxism is one theoretical paradigm structuring this representative selection of papers on Lessing presented at MLA meetings from 1971 through 1985, feminism is equally operative and equally plural. In proposing the story of Antigone as a female alternative to the Oedipal myth of (male) incestuous desire that Freud presented as universal, Elizabeth Abel participates in the revisionary project of feminist psychoanalytic criticism. Nicole Ward Jouve establishes a "French connection" for Lessing studies, as she ponders the contradiction between the "feminine" content of much of the Canopean series and its relentlessly nominative style, so different from the "female writing" of Helene Cixous, Marguerite Duras, or Clarice Lispector. In exploring the affinities between Doris Lessing and Olive Schreiner, Victoria Middleton contributes to the effort of feminist literary historians to re-member a female cultural tradition.

Middleton also discusses the particular situation of women within a colonial ruling class, a theme adumbrated in different ways by both Carey Kaplan and Lorna Sage. Both Schreiner and Lessing, Middleton writes, had "to come to terms with the cultures which gave them language to 'create' their own Africa but which also inscribed them as white women in a series of plots that diminished their potential." Lorna Sage emphasizes Lessing's dual status as "a Communist and a colonial—that is, a member of an oppositional minority within a dominant minority, neither of which acknowledged the positive meaning of race or gender." But although Middleton and, with some reservations, Sage represent Lessing as struggling against hegemonic (and patriarchal) colonialism, Kaplan accuses her of looking, in the Canopus series, "resolutely backwards into Britain's imperialist past" for "models of ideal behavior," thereby implicitly privileging the "stereotypically male" qualities of reason, order, and impersonality over the equally stereotypical female attributes of emotion, spontaneity, and the personal.

Questions of the personality (or impersonality) of the author preoccupy a number of the contributors to this book. Alvin Sullivan suggests that we are misguided if we seek to pin down "the author" who purposefully eludes us by "decentering" and "dispersing" authority in texts that, to paraphrase Lessing's remarks in the preface to *The Golden Notebook*, talk only through the way they are shaped. Lorna Sage, invoking Foucault on the author's refusal to die, counters that "the problem of decentering the author seems for Lessing so far insoluble." And Eve Bertelsen's brilliant analysis of the "discourse" of her interview with Lessing shows how strenuously *this* author works to control the reception and interpretation of her *oeuvre*.

Although by now you are probably eager to read the essays we have distilled from the lively ferment of Lessing panels at the last fifteen annual MLA conventions, we would like you to defer that pleasure in order to share our celebration of the tenacious vitality of a unique community of scholars, united—paradoxically—by their cordial, collegial tolerance of each other's different responses to a body of work that has changed lives as it has challenged the critical establishment.

2. A Genealogy of Readings

The Seventies

In 1971, Doris Lessing took up one and a half column inches in the MLA Bibliography. There was one book on Lessing—Dorothy Brewster's 1965 volume in the Twayne series—and two scholarly articles—Frederick P.W. McDowell's "The Fiction of Doris Lessing: An Interim View," in the 1965 volume of the *Arizona Quarterly*, and Selma R. Burkom's " 'Only Connect': Form and Content in the Works of Doris Lessing," in the 1968 volume of *Critique*. McDowell had also devoted several pages to Lessing in two review essays on "recent British fiction" in *Contemporary Literature*. James Gindin gave her a chapter in his 1962 *Postwar British Fiction*, but she merited only four pages in Bernard Bergonzi's *The Situation of the Novel* (1970) and a mere two pages in Frederick Karl's *A Reader's Guide to the Contemporary English Novel* (1963) and Walter Allen's *The Modern Novel in Britain and the United States* (1964).

So it took a considerable amount of scholarly chutzpah for Paul Schlueter to petition the MLA for permission to convene a seminar on "The Fiction of Doris Lessing" at the 1971 convention. "Lessing" at MLA meant Gottfried Lessing, the eighteenth-century German philosopher and aesthetician. It is a measure of the determination of Doris Lessing scholars in MLA that the eighteenth-century group now lists itself as the "G.E. Lessing" panel in the convention program, to distinguish itself from the two panels now annually devoted to the twentieth-century Lessing.

But the Lessing scholars who demanded a (seminar) room

of their own at the annual MLA convention are remarkable for more than their determination. As the following pages will demonstrate, they were harbingers of the central importance of Lessing both in any assessment of postwar British fiction and in developments in literary theory and critical practice during the last fifteen years.

Paul Schlueter opened MLA Seminar 46, the first MLA "special session" on Doris Lessing, by predicting that the "relatively tame" analysis of themes and topics he and other pioneering scholars had done on Lessing was about to be superseded by a "second generation" in Lessing studies. That the reins directing Lessing studies were changing hands was dramatically illustrated by the papers he'd selected for Seminar 46. Leonard Ashley's survey of the critical reception accorded *Children of Violence* demonstrated that traditional interpretive paradigms were incapable of appreciating Lessing's project. Readers whose idea of a central female protagonist had been shaped by Dorothea Brooke or Isabel Archer found Martha Quest boring, "too faceless and mindless to bear the burden of so many words."[13]

Furthermore, Lessing violated Jamesian principles of novel writing: she recorded everything, selected nothing. And generic critics were made so "ill at ease" by "a *Bildungsroman* in pieces" that they consigned *Children of Violence* to that lowest form of low culture, the soap opera. "Is there something more here," Ashley asked, than "Martha Faces Life, As the Stomach Turns, The Quest?" He concluded that there was, that *Children of Violence* should be regarded "as the 'notebooks' of a blocked writer," the crucible in which some ultimate golden notebook was being forged.

The forward trajectory of Ashley's paper is noteworthy. He could have chosen to discuss *The Golden Notebook* Lessing had already written. But although the popular imagination remained focused on that 1962 masterpiece, Lessing scholars were grappling with its aftermath: *Landlocked* (1965), *The Four-Gated City* (1969), and, most disturbingly, *Briefing for a Descent into Hell*, published just before MLA Seminar 46 convened in December 1971. The "new generation" scholarship Schlueter heralded in his introductory remarks brought to these innovative texts perspectives equally novel, derived from the late sixties' fascination with Eastern mysticism and antipsychiatry.

Briefing, for example, led both Selma Burkom and Lois Marchino to revisionist readings of Lessing's earlier fiction. Burkom's talisman was the city, whose "paradoxical" ground plan constitutes a mandala, Jung's archetypal image of wholeness attained through the reconciliation of opposites. Exploring this image in *The Golden Notebook* and *The Four-Gated City* as well as in *Briefing*, Burkom situated Lessing in the tradition, fusing German idealism and British romanticism, anticipated by Blake and most fully articulated by Coleridge. Burkom took Lessing a long way from soap opera.

But Marchino returned her to popular culture, by way of the currently fashionable existential psychiatry of R.D. Laing, whose Jesse Watkins in *The Politics of Experience* she proposed as a prototype for *Briefing*'s Charles Watkins. Like Burkom, Marchino read Lessing as the latest in a line of artists, philosophers, and mystics for whom the search for self entails a loss of self, for whom wholeness results from reconciling opposites.

If the 1971 seminar displayed the discrepancy between first- and second-generation Lessing scholars, the 1972 seminar suggested that part of the difference was sexual. The initial scholarship on Lessing was written by men: James Gindin, Frederick Karl, Frederick P.W. McDowell, John Carey, and Paul Schlueter. In 1972, only women submitted papers for the MLA Lessing seminar. And of the four essays chosen for presentation, three were overtly feminist in their approach to Lessing.

As feminism was infiltrating the academy in the early seventies, it should not be surprising to find it in Lessing studies. Mary Ellmann and Kate Millett had led the way in the late sixties, and in 1972 the first anthology of feminist criticism was published by Bowling Green University Popular Press, Susan Koppelman Cornillon's *Images of Women in Fiction: Feminist Perspectives*. Although Ellmann and Millett "resisted," to borrow Judith Fetterley's word,[14] the misogynist images of women in male-authored canonical texts, when feminist critics read women writers they looked for positive images, even "role models," asking with Martha Quest, "What does this say about my life?"

Early feminist criticism of Lessing belongs to this "images of women" school. Patricia Meyer Spacks characterized *The Golden Notebook* as "the book that *really* described the condition of the contemporary woman,[15] and Margaret Drabble called it a "document in the history of [women's] liberation."[16] At the MLA Seminar, Nancy Porter and Ellen Morgan had reservations, however. Morgan thought "the discrepancy between the perceptions [of women] and the alien standards which are imposed upon them" prevents *The Golden Notebook* from being that document in the history of women's liberation Drabble believed it was; she called it instead "a superb rendering" of the alienation from their own authentic experience that prefeminist women suffer. Nancy Porter shared Ellen Morgan's dual perspective on Lessing's achievement, praising her on the one hand for depicting the "silencing" of women's history, lamenting on the other Lessing's implicit suggestion in *The Four-Gated City* that "radical change" is accomplished ahistorically, "not in direct political action but in madness and mutation."

Of the 1972 panelists, only Annis Pratt applauded a "new feminism" that was at least "latent" in *The Golden Notebook*. Even so, Pratt included Morgan's more skeptical essay in the "Special Number on Doris Lessing" she coedited in 1973 for *Contemporary Literature* along with one by Sydney Janet Kaplan, who averred that in *The Four-Gated City* and *Briefing for a Descent into Hell*, the idea of a specifically "feminine" consciousness had "disintegrated." In these novels, Kaplan argued, "the idea of individual consciousness itself has been radically altered." Florence Howe, whose 1966 interview with Lessing was published for the first time in Pratt's special issue, hypothesized that "sometime before or during the writing of *The Four-Gated City*," a "shift" occurred in Lessing's work, registered for Howe by "a change in the political terms of the novel."[17] But other contributors to the Autumn 1973 issue of *Contemporary Literature* argued that Lessing's exploration of madness and mystical forms of transpersonal consciousness in *The Four-Gated City*, *Briefing* and *Jack Orkney* were as "political" as her earlier, more recognizably political analyses of class, race, and sex in southern Africa.

Yet the politics of the post-*Golden Notebook* fiction was undeniably different from the activities of Martha Quest's comrades in *A Ripple from the Storm* or Anna Wulf's Communist friends and associates in the Red Notebook. In 1973, the MLA special session on Lessing focused on "the politics of madness in Doris Lessing's novels." Roberta Rubenstein and Marion Vlastos Libby used the writings and practice of R.D. Laing to define what Libby called Lessing's "psychopolitics"; and while Frederick Stern tested her claims to being a Marxist, Jean Pickering attempted to connect the "politics of the left" with the "politics of madness" in Lessing's work.

The 1973 MLA panel developed the concern expressed by some contributors to *Contemporary Literature* with Lessing's (possibly changing) relation to politics. Nevertheless, John L. Carey's "Art and Reality in *The Golden Notebook*" was arguably the most influential essay in the Doris Lessing issue of *Contemporary Literature*, revolutionizing the way we read *The Golden Notebook*. It spawned a number of what might loosely be called "structural" readings of *The Golden Notebook* which emphasized its metafictional, self-reflexive qualities.

At the 1974 MLA Lessing panel, whose open-ended topic ("The Writing of Doris Lessing") elicited an eclectic group of papers, Valerie Carnes moved beyond formal considerations to ponder the thematic implications of the central role of art in *The Golden Notebook*. "Like the 'mousetrap' in *Hamlet* or Prospero's masque in *The Tempest*," she concluded, "the meta-novel, the novel-within-the-novel" is not only a "fictional device that puts black, red, yellow and blue notebooks and the 'Free Women' sections in their proper perspective," but it is also a demonstration of "the real efficacy of art" in contemporary society, representing "chaos" as something "ordered, salvaged, transformed," as Anna's life is, "by the alchemy of art."

The mythic paradigms of Jung, Campbell, and Frye suggest a different kind of "transformation," and Carol Christ adapted them to elucidate the particular dimensions of women's spiritual quest. Like Carol Christ, Sydney Janet Kaplan was fascinated by Lessing's use of the serial dream, with its invocation of an archetypal quest motif. But Kaplan insisted that "Doris Lessing puts Kate Brown's journey into a social, economic, biological, and political perspective." Similarly, Charlotte Solomon asserted that Lessing's treatment of mother-daughter relationships in *Children of Violence*, "takes the problem out of the realm of the personal, the individual" and "restates" it politically, "in terms of power structures and women's inability to formulate the truth about their experience and to communicate it to other women."

The 1974 Lessing special session ended with a student reading excerpts from the journal she had kept in Annis Pratt's course in "Recent British Fiction," recording her reactions to *The Golden Notebook*. This unorthodox conclusion to an MLA panel testified not only to the personal impact Lessing's novels make on most readers but also to a question that was beginning to vex scholars: how to *teach* Lessing, a question the 1975 panel on Lessing would explicitly consider.

With Annis Pratt's blessing, Sandra Curkeet had engaged in a dialogue with Lessing, questioning, arguing, protesting, even registering the effect being pregnant had on her response to the Martha Quest novels.[18] But, Martha Reid reported at the 1975 panel, when she had encouraged freshmen and sophomores at the College of William and Mary to "identify" with the Martha Quest of *A Proper Marriage*, she found to her dismay that they "identified so closely, yet so easily, so superficially with Martha Quest or her antagonists that they lost the distance necessary for insight." So when Reid next taught *A Proper Marriage*, she began with an outline of the book's structure and a list of important images. This "new critical" approach opened the way for substantive discussions of such themes as the relationship between marriage and war, fate, conflict between the generations, dreams, and the search for identity.

But Diane Gage challenged students and other readers to reconcile subjective and objective responses to Lessing's work, to retain the direct, felt first impression a novel like *Martha Quest* makes even as we critically "evaluate" it. Patsy Vigderman Goldberg's response was both subjective and negative. She found Lessing's early work "compelling because she was exposing old lies" but complained that from *The Four-Gated City* on, Lessing had staged a retreat from reality. As Dee Seligman noted in her introductory remarks, such views are "not usually found among the plaudits so common to a single-author seminar." But their inclusion typifies the MLA Lessing seminars, which have over the years both reflected and anticipated general critical response to Lessing.

In 1975, for example, the MLA seminar recognized —three years before Michael Thorpe published *Doris Lessing's Africa*—that Lessing must be considered an African novelist. Linda Susan Beard suggested that Africa was the source of Lessing's fiction, "the single fount both of the divisions with which Lessing's fiction abound and [of] the collective unity in which these separations are reconciled." Ranging freely over the stories and novels, Beard showed that the physical, cultural, political, and existential presence of Africa permeates Lessing's corpus, even when its setting is London.

By the mid-seventies, the entries under "Lessing, Doris" in the annual MLA Bibliography had swelled from the inch and a half they had occupied when the decade began to several columns. In 1976, Ellen Cronan Rose's monograph, *The Tree outside the Window*, joined Dorothy Brewster's *Doris Lessing* (1965), Paul Schlueter's *The Novels of Doris Lessing* (1973), and Michael Thorpe's *Doris Lessing* (1973). By the end of the decade, there would be three more book-length studies of Lessing: Mary Ann Singleton's *The City and the Veld* (1977), Michael Thorpe's *Doris Lessing's Africa* (1978), and Roberta Rubenstein's *The Novelistic Vision of Doris Lessing* (1979).

Chapters were devoted to Lessing in several landmark volumes of feminist literary criticism and history: Patricia Meyer Spacks's *The Female Imagination* (1975), Sydney Janet Kaplan's *Feminine Consciousness in the Modern British Novel* (1975), and Elaine Showalter's *A Literature of Their Own* (1977), whose subtitle highlighted Lessing's significance: *British Women Novelists from Bronte to Lessing*. Articles on Lessing appeared in such journals as *Studies in the Novel, Modern Fiction Studies, Critique,* the *Journal of Narrative Technique, World Literature Written in English,* the *Massachusetts Review* and *PMLA,* as well as in *Contemporary Literature*, which—as *Wisconsin Studies in Contemporary Literature*—had published Frederick P.W. McDowell's pioneering article on Lessing in 1963. And in 1976, Dee Seligman founded *The Doris Lessing Newsletter* to acknowledge and foster the "spirit of cooperation" which characterized MLA Lessing seminars.

Although most of the Lessing criticism published in the mid-seventies took up themes already adumbrated in MLA Lessing seminars—feminism, radical psychiatry, formal experimentation—some critics were beginning to situate Lessing in the context of science fiction, and a few turned their attention to her work in genres other than the novel. In 1976, the MLA Lessing seminar, too, turned from its exclusive focus on Lessing's novels to consider her short stories.

There are compelling reasons to consider Doris Lessing an African writer, Linda Beard asserted again, as she had in the previous year. Attention to her stories, in particular, reveals an attitude to time that owes more to indigenous African thought than to "the linear concept of time in western thought." Beard suggested that this "African" attitude to time also characterizes Lessing's novels, in which "process is the point."

Valerie Carnes made a point of re-reading *The Golden Notebook* (which she had approached from a different perspective in 1974) in view of what the stories encapsulated within it—many of them contained in the black notebook and based on African experience—reveal about Lessing's attitude toward "the limitations of conventional fictional forms." And both Patricia Chaffee and Betsy Draine treated Lessing's short story collections as Hugh Kenner had dealt with *Dubliners* in *Dublin's Joyce*, as "less a sequence of stories than a kind of multi-faceted novel."[19] The protagonists in Chaffee's novelistic reading of *African Stories* are groups of individuals segregated from each other in what Martha Quest would call "a sickness of dissolution."[20] This "society of closed systems" reminded Chaffee of Thomas Pynchon's "vision of entropy at work in human society."

Draine also found a "pattern" unifying apparently diverse stories to create the thematic spine of the volume. "In the widest sense"—a sense that includes but is not limited to the racial situation in southern Africa—"the stories are all about limits of vision, how they can be overcome, and how, if not overcome, they disease the eye." Draine concluded that Lessing is an Orwellian "political" novelist because, not content to remind us "of particular social injustices," she "reveals to us in fictional terms the limitations of vision and feeling that allow us to sanction injustice" and "shows us the possibility of a widened consciousness."

In 1977, Michael L. Magie announced in the respectable pages of *College English* that Doris Lessing was "worthy" of "being disagreed with" because "in her and through our responses to her we are working out our cultural destiny. . . . The question that she poses is whether we will emerge from the age of Romanticism at last and learn to live sanely and rationally on the unmade earth, or subside into the Decadence awaiting those who persist in delusions." The answer Magie arrives at—that "Lessing's novels . . . are now perhaps our best examples of decadent fiction"[21]—is less important than the route by which he gets there. Magie mounts his attack on Lessing by invoking the epistemological and ontological premises of (English) Romanticism, faulting her for abandoning the skepticism of Wordsworth for the prophetic enthusiasm of Blake and Shelley.

Nothing perhaps more clearly heralds a contemporary author's acceptance by the literary establishment than a critic's attempt to "place" him or her in a "tradition." Midway through our survey of Lessing's treatment by the academy, we encounter—in Magie's article, in Elaine Showalter's book on the "tradition" of British women novelists (and Lessing's place in that tradition), and at the 1977 MLA special session on Lessing, "Tradition and the Individual Talent"—a powerful urge to contain her, account for her, place her in some comprehensible (and teachable) context.

Yet, as the 1977 panel eloquently demonstrated, Lessing refused to be pigeonholed. Taking their cue from Lessing's statement in "The Small Personal Voice" that the "highest point of literature" was attained by "Tolstoy, Stendhal, Dostoevsky,

Balzac, Turgenev, Chekhov"; that "the realist novel, the realist story, is the highest form of prose writing: higher than and out of the reach of any comparison with expressionism, impressionism, symbolism, naturalism, or any other ism,"[22] Lorna Peterson and Terrell Dixon sought to lodge Lessing in that tradition, only to discover that she didn't comfortably fit. Peterson singled out Dostoevsky from the pantheon Lessing had erected in "The Small Personal Voice" because his brand of realism seemed to fit the Lessing who had moved away from the documentary realism of the early Martha Quest novels to the visionary, even apocalyptic *Four-Gated City*, *Briefing for a Descent into Hell*, and *The Memoirs of a Survivor*. But despite the uncanny parallels between *Briefing* and Dostoevsky's "Dream of a Ridiculous Man" Peterson uncovered, she concluded that the differences between the two authors are even more significant. "For Lessing there can be no individual salvation without political awareness. . . . Even though Lessing's later protagonists make ever more penetrating journeys into the interior they are . . . still concerned with pushing boulders."

Terrell Dixon, who also saw affinities between Lessing and Dostoevsky, agreed with Peterson that "to say that in *Briefing for a Descent into Hell* Lessing abandons the realistic novel for the apocalyptic mode is to misinterpret" her. But, taking a cue from Kate Brown's "disdainful" response in *The Summer before the Dark* to a performance of Chekhov's *A Month in the Country*, he suggested that the nineteenth century's brand of realism might not be Lessing's. He proposed, instead, to approach Lessing by way of the "new realism" of Alain Robbe-Grillet and Nathalie Sarraute, with whom—as he demonstrated—Lessing shares many techniques of characterization, plotting, and self-reflexiveness.

Nancy Topping Bazin and Judith Stitzel steered between the Scylla of nineteenth-century realism and the Charybdis of the French new novel in readings that aligned Lessing instead with the classic modernists. Bazin set Martha Quest's moment of "illumination" on the veld beside comparable moments of "revelation" or "epiphany" in Lawrence and Joyce, and Stitzel considered the larger context in which such "moments" occur, the modernists' compelling desire to represent consciousness realistically (and verbally). Terrell Dixon turned to contemporary French fiction to understand Lessing's brand of realism; Judith Stitzel suspected that Jacques Lacan's semiotic revision of Freud would "contribute importantly" to further study of Lessing's narrative technique (a prediction that has yet to be fulfilled).

Neither the MLA nor Doris Lessing is known for a sense of humor, but one pair of papers presented at the 1977 Lessing special session provides retrospective amusement, if not a belly laugh. Mildred Sarah Greene and Virginia Tiger agreed that Lessing belonged to a novelistic tradition grounded in the eighteenth rather than the nineteenth or twentieth century, but they proposed antithetical traditions. Greene traced a direct line from the Princess of Cleves to Clarissa Harlowe to Anna Wulf, all "heroines of integrity" belonging to "the novelistic tradition of sensibility or psychological self-analysis." Tiger called Anna Wulf, rather, a "confessional heroine" in the tradition of Mary Wollstonecraft, who chooses sense ("the individual's right to *responsible* liberty") over sensibility ("the worship of self"). As the session broke up, those who had attended hoping to discover where to "place" Lessing might well have pondered the words of *Briefing*'s Charles Watson, "It isn't either/or, it's and, and, and, and . . ."[23]

Nevertheless, because Lessing had produced no fiction since the 1975 publication of *The Memoirs of a Survivor*, whose dust jacket description as "an attempt at autobiography" had a valedictory ring, scholars felt obliged to take stock of what looked like a finished corpus. Speakers at the 1978 MLA special session on Lessing tried again to "place" Lessing, this time in a specifically twentieth-century context of visionary writing.

In a series of readings comparing Lessing to George Orwell, Ursula K. LeGuin, and Aldous Huxley, panelists repeatedly characterized Lessing's recent fiction as "visionary," "mystical," "religious." The argument implicit in Claire Sprague's paper—that the "ability to contain and burst boundaries and oppositions" and thus achieve an integrative "vision" is psychological and private rather than political and social—was made explicit by Mary LeDonne, who said that "the real key to survival" for Lessing is not political but personal, even subjective: "each individual's ability and willingness to heal himself or herself."

Although her fellow panelists spoke positively, even admiringly, of Lessing's "mystical" or "visionary" strain, Victoria Middleton called *Memoirs of a Survivor* a "consolatory escape from, rather than a confrontation with, contingent reality." According to Middleton, Lessing had not "matured" or "developed" (as Leslie Gerber and Margaret McFadden-Gerber had implied) but entered her dotage: "*The Memoirs of a Survivor* is a work that dramatizes what Freud calls [in *The Future of an Illusion*] the desire to 'remain a child for ever.'"

In 1979, to the dismay of Lessing loyalists, the MLA Program Committee rejected—for the first time since 1971—a proposal for a special session on Lessing. Yet during that year when "nothing happened" (officially) at MLA, three events occurred that changed the course of Lessing studies. A major university press published Roberta Rubenstein's book on Lessing, thus implicitly ceding her status as a subject for serious academic inquiry. A Doris Lessing Society was formed as an Allied Organization of the MLA, thus guaranteeing not one but two Lessing panels at succeeding conventions. And with the publication of *Re: Colonized Planet Five, Shikasta,* Lessing embarked on a sequence of novels that would eventually rival *Children of Violence* in length and radically challenge all tentative conclusions reached in the seventies about Lessing's "place" in one tradition or another.

THE EIGHTIES

AFTER THE UNWELCOME BUT PRODUCTIVE HIATUS of 1979, the newly formed Doris Lessing Society returned to the December 1980 MLA convention with renewed energy. Indeed, 1980 was a banner year for Lessing scholarship. Two book-length studies of Lessing were published by European scholars, the first indication that Lessing studies were going international.[24] *Modern*

Fiction Studies brought out a special issue on Lessing, featuring essays by former MLA panelists.[25] There were chapters or essays on Lessing in three books on women and literature,[26] and articles on Lessing appeared in eight journals in addition to *Modern Fiction Studies*.

Writing in the *Doris Lessing Newsletter*, Jean Pickering called *The Golden Notebook* a "watershed between realism and whatever else we may choose to label Lessing's style, techniques, themes, interests, and generic bents in the past twenty years."[27] Articles by Jean Bethke Elshtain and Patrick Parrinder had lamented Lessing's new direction (Elshtain called Lessing a "prophet" who had "repudiated history" in her "eschatological zeal" for millennial renovation, and Parrinder said her "small personal voice" had become "a scriptural voice, crying in a wilderness of her own choosing").[28] But contributors to the *Modern Fiction Studies* special issue and panelists at the 1980 MLA convention were more interested in blending vintage Lessing (from *The Grass Is Singing* through *The Golden Notebook*) with the new wine of what Lessing called "space fiction" in the preface to *Shikasta*. To do so, they employed new theoretical and critical apparatuses.

For the first time, the announcement of the MLA panels in the winter issue of the *Doris Lessing Newsletter* suggested some preliminary "Recommended Readings," including such hitherto unheard of glosses on Lessing as Wolfgang Iser, Pierre Macherey, and Umberto Eco. It was heady stuff for an audience reared on Blake, Jung, and Laing. Yet what the new approaches to Lessing were attempting to discern was continuity between the familiar realism of the early fiction and the prophetic, cosmological mode of the newer novels. From Marie Ahearn to Roswell Spafford, the panelists iterated their conviction that Lessing's space fiction was concerned, no less than *Children of Violence*, with the study "of the individual conscience in its relations with the collective."[29] Despite her excursion into outer space, panelists maintained, Doris Lessing remained preeminently a political novelist, simultaneously symptomatic and critical of contemporary ideologies and social relationships.

At the same time, the special Lessing issue of *Modern Fiction Studies* indicated that critical attention was clearly shifting (as it had begun to do as early as Carey's article on *The Golden Notebook*) from what Bernard Duyfhuizen, quoting Tsvetan Todorov, identified as the "story" (*histoire*) of the novels to the "story of their writing" (their *discours*).[30] Lessing's fiction was becoming less interesting to critics than her writing of it and our reading(s).

Twice in the past twenty years, major journals have devoted special issues to Doris Lessing. These ventures have attracted new, often male, critics to a corpus of works that have for the most part been read and championed by women. Both the 1973 special Lessing issue of *Contemporary Literature* and the 1980 Lessing issue of *Modern Fiction Studies* presented Doris Lessing as a major contemporary novelist, whose gender was if not irrelevant at least not the most salient factor in evaluating her achievement. In 1981, as in 1974, this effort to bring Lessing into the canonical mainstream was followed by a countereffort to reclaim her for a specifically "female tradition." The spate of 1980 articles situating Lessing in a variety of sexless traditions (modernist, postmodernist, romantic, utopian, visionary, crackpot) was followed, in 1981, by an MLA panel which asked whether she belonged in "the great tradition" or "the female tradition," and answered resoundingly that, no matter what she said, Doris Lessing was constitutively female.

Jean Pickering placed Lessing in the line of women writers identified by Sandra Gilbert and Susan Gubar in *The Madwoman in the Attic: The Woman Writer and the Nineteenth Century Literary Imagination*[31] who "fragment" or "double" their female persona into a good woman and a madwoman "to express the deep division forced on the woman writer by the patriarchal culture." But although nineteenth-century women writers "always implicitly recommended some kind of authorial compromise with the patriarchal establishment," Pickering suggested that after Lessing "such a compromise may no longer be possible" because her "madwoman is out of attic and basement and powerfully loosed upon the world."[32]

Elizabeth Abel agreed that Lessing was revolutionary but argued that "while Lessing shares concerns and values with her British female predecessors, her play with form in *The Golden*

Notebook distances her from a female tradition defined primarily through recurrent themes, images, plots, and characters." Instead, Abel placed Lessing in the French tradition of *ecriture feminine* because "Anna translates her frustrated political desires into a radical literary practice." It is the *form* of *The Golden Notebook* that marks it female. "By suggesting formlessness through form," Anna's novel not only challenges the system of binary oppositions patriarchy has constructed around the basic division "male/female," but also arises from her biological experience of womanhood (That's how women see things," she tells Tommy. "Everything in a sort of continuous creative stream—well, isn't it natural we should?").[33] Earlier in 1981, Abel had used the feminist psychoanalytic theories of Nancy Chodorow and Dorothy Dinnerstein[34] to explore the empowering effect on Anna Wulf's and Martha Quest's development of their relationships with women.[35] Thus, by the end of 1981, Lessing had been "claimed" by the three leading schools of feminist literary theory represented by Gilbert and Gubar, *ecriture feminine*, and revisionary psychoanalysis.

Two of the speakers at the 1981 panel on "Teaching Doris Lessing" considered the implications of incorporating female writing within the patriarchal structures of the academy and the literary canon. Nancy Grayson welcomed the preface to *The Golden Notebook*, which "questions the whole critical enterprise," into her survey of literary criticism because it "jars" students "into noticing distinctions" between subsequent assignments and "encourages" them "to think independently." Grayson's only fear was that by adding Lessing's preface to her syllabus she might thereby domesticate Lessing; the problem was how to "teach Lessing's protest without integrating it into the 'literary machine' she so dislikes."

Although Grayson celebrated the disruptive effect of adding Lessing to the patriarchal canon, Martha Satz asked what *The Golden Notebook* does to our notions of "feminist writing." *The Golden Notebook* forces students and teacher alike to confront what Satz called the "real issues" of feminist fiction: "What areas of experience, conversation, and perception are distinctively feminine? Should a feminist novel be descriptive or prescriptive? What solutions may such a novel propose or advocate? Do peculiarly feminine literary structures exist?" In other words, dealing with contradictions in this "ambiguously feminist" text forces students to "confront" the "conceptual and personal" issues involved in constructing a theory of women's writing.

Efforts to situate Lessing in a female tradition continued at the 1982 MLA convention. At the panel on "Doris Lessing and the Female Tradition," Leah Ogden elaborated one strand of Jean Pickering's 1981 paper on "The Anguish of Feminine Fragmentation" to emphasize the transformation, in the Martha Quest novels, of the traditionally "vital" and "wholistic" archetype of the circle into a (biological) cycle of "appalling fatality" ("the nightmare repetition"). She was followed by Linda Bamber, who viewed Lessing's movement away from the linear plot structure of tragedy toward the cyclic form of romance more positively. Bamber discerned in Lessing's fiction a pattern found in one tradition of women's writing, in which "the female narrator and certain representative characters survive or encompass tragic experience" through a "shift in consciousness" which places loss and suffering in a new perspective. In fact, Bamber argued, this female tradition (represented by George Eliot, Virginia Woolf, Grace Paley, Flannery O'Connor, and Eudora Welty, as well as Doris Lessing) *refuses* tragedy, the "great central prestigious Western masculine form," preferring continuance to apocalypse, "survival through a change in consciousness."

Did Lessing belong to a female tradition of victimization or of survival? To neither, Ellen Cronan Rose suggested, arguing rather that the central trope of her fiction from *Martha Quest* through *Shikasta*, the fabulous four-gated city, allied Lessing to a tradition with "no female exemplars." For the radial design of Martha's ideal city resembles not only the Jungian mandala —as Roberta Rubenstein, Mary Ann Singleton, and others had pointed out—but also the *citta felice* of Italian renaissance architects. Read in light of that tradition, Lessing's city becomes a model of a unified self whose ontological security depends on a religious metaphysics which erases not only sexuality but also individuality. What "survives" in the Canopus novels is an impersonal and collective "essence," represented most fully in *The Making of the Representative for Planet 8*.

Similarly, although three of the speakers at the 1982 panel on "Doris Lessing and the Commonwealth Novel" compared Lessing to female commonwealth novelists, they were not primarily concerned with gender. Although Katherine Fishburn contrasted Buchi Emecheta's "domestic feminist perspective" to Lessing's "apocalyptic and galactic perspective," she emphasized their common critique of repressive conservative traditions, colonial for Lessing, native Igbo for the Nigerian Emecheta. The focus of Linda Weinhouse's and Virginia Tiger's papers was less on the shared femaleness of Doris Lessing, Isak Dinesen, and Janet Frame than on their experience and representation of exile. And Linda Susan Beard used *The Golden Notebook* to elucidate the (male) Ghanaian Ayi Kwei Armah's "complex novel of signs," *Fragments* (1971).

In the same year that U.S. scholars were situating Lessing in a commonwealth context, a commonwealth journal devoted a substantial section of one issue to her work,[36] and an important collection of essays on Lessing by English, Anglo-French, and Australian critics was published simultaneously in Boston and London.[37] A review of *Notebooks/Memoirs/Archives: Reading and Rereading Doris Lessing* for the *Doris Lessing Newsletter* noted that for the most part "American critics have failed to take sufficient note of the political and ideological sources of Lessing's early commitment to realism" and suggested that "in this area, we have much to learn from our British Marxist-feminist colleagues" (7, no.1 [Summer 1983]: 5-6, 10). In December 1983, Jenny Taylor, the book's editor, brought her Marxist feminist reading of *Going Home* to New York, where for the first time foreign scholars participated in an MLA Lessing session, on "Doris Lessing and Africa."

Like Taylor, the South African Eve Bertelsen also proposed a deconstructive Marxist model for "understanding Lessing's literary version of Africa," encoded in *The Grass Is Singing, African Stories*, and *Children of Violence*. Bertelsen discerned three "basic discourses" at work in these texts: history, *bildung*, and myth. Rather than choosing one of these as "dominant" in a given text, Bertelsen examined the way in which Lessing "displaces an initial 'factual' or metonymic depiction of Rhodesia through a series of 'poetic' strategies into timeless myth." In a brief but suggestive coda, Bertelsen used her "map" of Lessing's African fiction to get at its underlying *raison d'être*, concluding that "the twin poles of Lessing's discourse" are "determinism and Romance" and that "her fiction effects an ideological reconciliation between the two."

If one of the 1983 panels had an international flavor, the other was designedly intergalactic, focusing on "Strategies for Reading *Canopus in Argos*." Following Lessing's clue, in "Some Remarks" prefatory to *Shikasta*, that Olaf Stapledon's *Last and First Men* figured importantly in her construction of the Canopean empire, Robert Shelton traced Lessing's possible debts to Stapledon and Arthur C. Clarke, his heir and admirer, but Robin Roberts insisted that Lessing transcended Stapledon's "androcentric model." Roberts read *Canopus in Argos* as an "ambitious work of feminist science fiction," whose prototype was not Stapledon's *The Star Maker* but Mary Shelley's *Frankenstein*. More comprehensively than her sister science fiction writers, Roberts maintained, Lessing "reclaims the genre" to "revise female myths of power," using science fiction as "future sociology."

Jeffrey Steele looked further back in history for the source of Lessing's cosmology and proposed the syncretic gnosticism of Alexandrian Greece as "a compendium of images and doctrines feeding into both Sufism and Jungian psychology" and, through them, into Lessing's space fiction. Reading *Shikasta* as a "gnostic epic" enabled Steele to account both for Lessing's "organizing myth" and for her "literary use of this visionary material," which becomes more than a simple "paradigm for self-realization." In Lessing's hands, gnosis leads to a new, visionary politics: "the horizon of her recent fiction delimits more than the expanse of individual vision; it bounds a circle of potential consciousness which might include the whole human race."

Certainly the circle of critical consciousness about Lessing had expanded, by the mid-eighties, from its parochial beginnings in the 1971 inaugural MLA Lessing seminar to include, if not the whole human race, at least "representatives" from other continents and theoretical discourses. Jenny Taylor returned in December 1984 to chair one of two panels devoted to the intersections of politics and ideology in Lessing's fiction. British scholars set the tone for that year's discussion, but paradoxically, they sounded a French note, invoking Julia Kristeva, Hélène Cixous, and Roland Barthes in their attempts to position Lessing's politics and narrative practice from *African Stories* through the just-published *Diaries of Jane Somers*.

In her discussion of *African Stories*, Clare Hanson connected the themes of exile and colonization directly to two narrative modes Lessing herself identified as "masculine" and "feminine." Lessing's "masculine" prose, as Hanson analyzes it, is "a language of selection, excision, expropriation," in short, of "colonization." What, then, are we to make of Lessing's stated preference for "masculine" writing? Hanson thought "it could be argued that in writing about a colonial system she wholeheartedly deplores, Lessing nevertheless reproduces or perpetuates in the processes of some of these texts patriarchal, and by extension colonial, systems and values."[38] The constellation of ideas in Hanson's paper—gendered style, exile, colonialism—were teased out and elaborated in three papers we have included in this book, by Nicole Ward Jouve, Carey Kaplan, and Lorna Sage.

One of the 1985 MLA panels seized on a theme that ran through the 1984 papers, that—as Susan Greenstein would put it—there is "an overarching thematic unity in Lessing's work over a thirty-year period." The call for papers suggested that "during a writing career which has developed from regional to global to cosmic and from personal to political to transpersonal, Doris Lessing has returned again and again to the dynamic of the life cycle," and that it was "tempting to hypothesize" that this obsession might have roots in Lessing's autobiography. In Chicago that December, panelists accounted for the developmental curve of Lessing's fiction in terms of her working through a problematic relationship with her mother. Eva Hunter contrasted the cautionary lesson of *The Grass Is Singing*, that the daughter who fails to separate from her mother is doomed to destruction, to the celebration of maternity in *The Marriages between Zones Three, Four, and Five* and suggested that it indicated a change in Lessing's attitude toward her own mother, citing as evidence Lessing's acknowledgment that her mother lay behind her (positive) portrayal of Jane Somers. Gayle Greene concentrated on the Jane Somers novels, suggesting that "the use of the pseudonym allowed her to deal with matters she could not confront as Doris Lessing—still-cathected matters related to the mother." Arguing that, in the main, Lessing's "return to the unresolved mother-daughter relationship" of the Martha Quest novels in *The Diaries* is positive, Greene nonetheless had reservations. The "geniality" and "mellowness" of these novels, "which suggest a relaxation of an earlier guardedness related in part to [Lessing's] mother" are possible only because Lessing has "forgotten" the "connections between personal and political." The novels retrieve "personal sentiment at the expense of political analysis."

Judith Kegan Gardiner also connected the mother-daughter dynamic in Lessing's fiction with her attitudes toward history and politics, specifically with "the hope for positive historical change." Unlike Greene, she found both "vital anger" and "modest social optimism" in at least the first of the Jane Somers novels. But *The Good Terrorist*, published in 1985, "regresses" from both the mother/daughter reconciliation of *The Diaries* and a belief in constructive political action.

The Good Terrorist and *The Diaries of Jane Somers* were very much on people's minds in December 1985 in large part because Lessing had put them there. The reclusive author who had counseled younger writers in 1963, "Don't review, don't go on television, try to keep out of all that," who thought it was "better to try and remain what we should be—an individual who communicates with other individuals, through the written word,"[39] became a media event in 1984. The notorious leg-pull by which Lessing hoaxed not only the common reader but also critics and reviewers into "overlooking" two new Lessing novels because they were signed "Jane Somers" was strategically "confessed" in the introduction to *The Diaries of Jane Somers*, repackaged as a Vintage paperback by Doris Lessing, whose sales more than compensated for the losses Knopf sustained in publishing the "unknown" Jane Somers. Immediately thereafter, Lessing embarked on an extensive lecture tour of the United States and Canada, capped by the interview with Susan Stamberg on "All Things Considered" from which we quoted earlier. What was she up to? Two speakers at the 1985 MLA Lessing panels defined the politics of Lessing's authorial intervention into the reception and evaluation of her *oeuvre*. Elizabeth Maslen's and Eve Bertelsen's papers suggested that our reading of Lessing has been less "scholarly" and "objective" than we like to believe; that it has, in fact, been engineered all along by her imperatives.

Maslen argued that Lessing had been "teasingly exploiting" the relationship "between her novels' narrative voices and her readers" throughout her thirty-year career, thus foiling critical attempts to locate "a single, certain statement of authorial intent." She generously attributed this game to Lessing's epistemological rigor; what it suggested to her was that Lessing was forcing her readers to "probe" their "definitions of omniscience," jolting them to "engage fully" with the meaning of the text in order to recognize their complicity in its production. Bertelsen was more skeptical, noting Lessing's extratextual attempt to "fix" the meaning of her *oeuvre*, her manipulation of critical response by "granting" interviews selectively in order to establish "authorial control" over our readings.

We conclude our fifteen-year survey of Lessing scholarship with Bertelsen's essay because it suggests—as do the topics for the 1986 MLA Lessing seminars[40]—that what we have now to do with is an "author," rather than some texts a variety of readers have found meaningful, troublesome, stimulating, even life-changing. From 1971, when Paul Schlueter dared to propose an MLA seminar on the "popular" novelist Doris Lessing to 1986 when the MLA officially recognized *The Golden Notebook* as a "Masterpiece of World Literature,"[41] Lessing scholarship has taken a giant step, comparable to Lessing's own leap from Africa to Argos and beyond. This volume documents the journey and asks the reader to judge whether she, and we, have grown in the process.

NOTES

1. Susan Stamberg, "An Interview with Doris Lessing," reprinted in *Doris Lessing Newsletter* 8, no. 2 (Fall 1984): 3-4, 15.

2. Jacques Derrida, *Speech and Phenomena: And Other Essays on Husserl's Theory of Signs*, trans. David B. Allison (Evanston, Ill.: Northwestern University Press, 1973), 130. See also Allison's appended translation of Derrida's essay "La Differance" (1968).

3. Idries Shah, *The Sufis* (New York: Doubleday & Co., 1971).

4. John Carey to the editors, 27 Nov. 1985.

5. Lisa Alther, in conversation with the editors, November 1985.

6. Despite Julia Kristeva's suggestion that the gestural, rhythmic, and preferential language of male modernists like Joyce, Mallarme, and Artaud signals eruptions from the pre-Oedipal, maternal "semiotic" into the "symbolic" register dominated by the law of the Father, we still maintain that the self-consciousness of this language gives it a quality of abstraction that distinguishes it from the solid, grounded writing of Lessing. See Kristeva, *Desire in Language: A Semiotic Approach to Literature and Art*, ed. Leon S. Roudiez (New York: Columbia University Press, 1980) esp. chaps. 3, 6 and 7, pp. 64-91, 148-209.

7. Carey letter, 27 Nov. 1985.

8. Frederick P.W. McDowell to the editors, March 1986.

9. Carey letter, 27 Nov. 1985.

10. Dee Seligman, "Statement of Purpose," *Doris Lessing Newsletter* 1, no. 1 (Winter 1976): 2.

11. Dee Seligman to the editors, 12 March 1986.

12. Paul Schlueter to the editors, 14 Feb. 1986.

13. Leonard Ashley was quoting from Rosemary Neiswender's review of *Children of Violence*, vol. 1 (*Martha Quest* and *A Proper Marriage*) in *Library Journal* 89 (15 Dec. 1964): 4932.

14. Judith Fetterley, *The Resisting Reader: A Feminist Approach to American Fiction* (Bloomington: Indiana University Press, 1978).

15. Patricia Meyer Spacks, "Free Women," *Hudson Review* 24 (Winter 1971-72): 559-73.

16. Margaret Drabble, "Doris Lessing: Cassandra in a World under Siege," *Ramparts* 10 (February 1972): 50-54.

17. See *Contemporary Literature* 14 (Autumn 1973): 537,420. This issue was reprinted as *Doris Lessing: Critical Studies*, ed. Annis Pratt and L.S. Dembo (Madison: University of Wisconsin Press, 1974).

18. Patricia Meyer Spacks's *The Female Imagination* (New York: Avon, 1975) draws on similarly engaged responses to a range of women's texts by students in Spacks's Wellesley College freshman-sophomore literature colloquium.

19. Hugh Kenner, *Dublin's Joyce* (Bloomington: Indiana University Press, 1956), x. See also Brewster Ghiselin, "The Unity of Joyce's *Dubliners*," in the Viking Critical *Dubliners*, ed. Robert Scholes and A. Walton Litz (New York: The Viking Press, 1969), 316-32.

20. Doris Lessing, *Martha Quest* (1952; reprint, New York: New American Library, 1964), 47.

21. Michael L. Magie, "Doris Lessing and Romanticism," *College English* 38, no. 6 (February 1977): 531, 552. See Judith Stitzel's rebuttal in "Reading Doris Lessing," *College English* 40 (January 1979): 498-504.

22. Doris Lessing, *A Small Personal Voice: Essays, Reviews, Interviews*, ed. Paul Schlueter (New York: Alfred A. Knopf, 1974), 4.

23. Doris Lessing, *Briefing for a Descent into Hell* (New York: Alfred A. Knopf, 1971), 140.

24. Rotraut Spiegel, *Doris Lessing: The Problem of Alienation and the Form of the Novel* (Frankfurt: Verlag Peter D. Lang, 1980); and Ingrid Holmquist, *From Society to Nature: A Study of Doris Lessing's Children of Violence* (Goteberg, Sweden: Acta Universitatis Gothoburgensis, 1980).

25. "Doris Lessing Number," *Modern Fiction Studies* 26, no. 1 (Spring 1980). See the essays by Nancy Topping Bazin, Betsy Draine, Jean Pickering, Dee Seligman, and Claire Sprague.

26. Carol P. Christ, *Diving Deep and Surfacing: Women Writers on Spiritual Quest* (Boston: Beacon Press, 1980); Cathy N. Davidson and E.M. Broner, eds., *The Lost Tradition* (New York: Ungar, 1980); Carol Landau Heckerman, ed., *The Evolving Female* (New York: Human Sciences Press, 1980).

27. Jean Pickering, "Strategies for Reading Lessing," *Doris Lessing Newsletter* 5, no. 1 (Summer 1981): 3.

28. Jean Bethke Elshtain, "The Post-*Golden Notebook* Fiction of Doris Lessing," *Salmagundi* 47-48 (Winter-Spring 1980): 95-114; and Patrick Parrinder, "Descents into Hell: The Later Novels of Doris Lessing," *Critical Quarterly* 22 (Winter 1980): 5-25.

29. Lessing, *Small Personal Voice*, 14.

30. Bernard Duyfhuizen, "On the Writing of Future-History: Beginning the Ending in Doris Lessing's *The Memoirs of A Survivor*," *Modern Fiction Studies* 26, no. 1 (Spring 1980): 147-56.

31. Sandra Gilbert and Susan Gubar, *The Madwoman in the Attic: The Woman Writer and the Nineteenth-Century Literary Imagination* (New Haven: Yale University Press, 1979).

32. Jean Pickering, "Martha Quest and the 'Anguish of Female Fragmentation,' " in *Critical Essays on Doris Lessing*, ed. Claire Sprague and Virginia Tiger (Boston: G.K. Hall, 1986), 94-100.

33. Elizabeth Abel, "*The Golden Notebook*: 'Female Writing' and 'The Great Tradition,' " in *Critical Essays on Doris Lessing*, ed. Claire Sprague and Virginia Tiger (Boston: G.K. Hall, 1986), 101-07.

34. Nancy Chodorow, *The Reproduction of Mothering: Psychoanalysis and the Sociology of Gender* (Berkeley: University of California Press, 1978); and Dorothy Dinnerstein, *The Mermaid and the Minotaur: Sexual Arrangements and Human Malaise* (New York: Harper & Row, 1976).

35. Elizabeth Abel, "(E)Merging Identities: The Dynamics of Female Friendship in Contemporary Fiction by Women," *Signs* 6, no. 3 (Spring 1981): 413-35.

36. *World Literature Written in English* 21, no. 3 (Autumn 1982): 411-67.

37. Jenny Taylor, ed., *Notebooks/Memoirs/Archives: Reading and Rereading Doris Lessing* (Boston and London: Routledge & Kegan Paul, 1982).

38. Clare Hanson, "The Woman Writer as Exile: Gender and Possession in the African Stories of Doris Lessing." in *Critical Essays on Doris Lessing*, ed. Claire Sprague and Virginia Tiger (Boston: G.K. Hall, 1986). 107-14.

39. Lessing, *Small Personal Voice*, 53.

40. Virginia Tiger's and Claire Sprague's topics are "Doris Lessing: Autobiographical Encodings" and "Doris Lessing in Europe and Africa: The Critical Reception."

41. Carey Kaplan and Ellen Cronan Rose have been invited to prepare a volume on *The Golden Notebook* for the MLA series, *Approaches to Teaching Masterpieces of World Literature*.

Selected Essays

Frederick C. Stern

Doris Lessing: The Politics of Radical Humanism

Doris Lessing is certainly an intensely political writer and especially so in her earlier work. Indeed, the subject matter of her novels—from *The Grass Is Singing* through the last volume of her five-novel work, *Children of Violence*, *The Golden Notebook*, and some subsequent volumes—is, in large part, the politics of the periods through which her characters live. The subject is not so much the detail of the political process, as one finds it sometimes in C.P. Snow or in such an American novelist as Edwin O'Connor, but rather the social and political world view, the expressed or implied social philosophy of her characters, and the personal ramifications of that world view for them.

In this sense, then, Lessing performs well—sometimes brilliantly—precisely one of the major tasks of the work of fiction prescribed by Georg Lukacs, in his well-know essay, "The Intellectual Physiognomy of Literary Characters." Lukacs writes that

> in all great writing it is indispensable that its characters be depicted in all-sided interdependence with each other, with their social existence, and with the great problems of this existence. The more deeply these relations are grasped, the more diversely these interconnections are developed, the greater the writing becomes, for the closer it comes to the actual richness of life. . . .

> A description that does not include the *Weltanschauung* of the created characters cannot be complete. *Weltanschauung* is the highest form of consciousness; hence, if the writer ignores it he blurs the most important thing in the figure he has in mind. *Weltanschauung* is a profound personal experience of each and every person, an extremely characteristic expression of his inward nature, and it likewise reflects in a very significant fashion the general problems of his age.[1]

[As I re-examine my essay, first written in 1973, I am much more aware than I was then how debatable Lukacs's dictum is. Its implication that literature is, self-evidently, mimetic; its assumption that the expressed "world view" (the term I will use to translate *Weltanschauung*, though it is really not quite adequate) of a character can be readily taken at face value—these and other difficulties arise in the light of poststructuralist criticism. Nevertheless, it seems to me, there is still utility in applying Lukacs's term to Lessing's work, precisely *because* she is so determinedly a political writer in the works under discussion here. Another paper might well be written—although I doubt that it could have been written, and it certainly could not have been written by me, in 1973—which would raise other, more "poststructuralist" questions about Lessing's work.][2]

It seems to me quite clear that the major characters of *Children of Violence*, of *Retreat to Innocence*, and of *The Golden Notebook*, that is, of Lessing's most crucial novel-length fiction up to 1965, are given precisely such a world view to express, although the kinds of views expressed change and vary as the novels develop. Indeed, her world view and the way Martha Quest changes in this regard is, in one sense, the matter of *Children of Violence*; a difference in world view between the two major characters, Julia Barr and Jan Brod, is the matter of *Retreat to Innocence*; the quest for a viable world view in face of the loss of an older one is the matter of *The Golden Notebook*.

Most interesting to me are two aspects of Lessing's earlier work, as it concerns the changing world view of her characters. The first of these has to do with the change in form which seems to accompany changes in the characters' world view; the second aspect has to do with the ideological premises of the changes in point of view of her major characters. In order to explore these two problems, it will be necessary to examine briefly some of the changes in world view which Lessing's characters undergo, not only for each character individually, but also as reflected in the *corpus*[3] of Lessing's work, from *Martha Quest*, through *The Four-Gated City*.

Martha Quest and *A Proper Marriage*, the first two novels in the *Children of Violence* quintet, show us the development of a protagonist who finds in the ideology of the Communist party of the middle and late 1940s a rationale for living. Martha escapes control from her petit-bourgeois family by leaving the farm and goes through a brief and unhappy flirtation with the social life of the big city and through her first affair. At about the same time during this period, she discovers the radical movement and enters into marriage, thus feeling herself rescued from the futility, the emptiness of a life-style characterized by "sundowner" cocktail parties. She now becomes fully conscious, in part through her contact with Communists and Socialists, of the terrible impact of racism on her society, finds explanations from the "movement" for her dissatisfaction with her marriage to the hapless Douglas Knowell, and thus leaves her marriage, even her daughter Caroline, "liberating" herself in order to devote full-time to "the party." Her conversation with Mr. Maynard, perhaps the most intelligent representative of the world view of the rulers of the Zambesian society in which she lives, makes clear, at the end of *A Proper Marriage*, the point at which Martha had arrived.

> "Deserting?" he enquired.
>
> "Quite so."
>
> "You look extraordinarily pleased about it." It was true, she was now so elated she felt light as an air bubble. "Well, what are you going to do now?"
>
> She misunderstood him and said, "I'm going to drop my things in my room, look for a job, and then —there are five hundred envelopes to be addressed before tomorrow morning." She said it as if describing the heights of human bliss.

Maynard's subsequent comment, and Martha's reply, sum up Martha's present feeling state: " 'I suppose with the French Revolution for a father and the Russian Revolution for a mother, you can very well dispense with a family'. . . ." After a while she conceded, " 'That is really a very intelligent remark.' "[4]

The first discernible shift from such whole-hearted immersion in the Communist party's position can be found in *Retreat to Innocence*, published in 1956, after *Martha Quest* and *A Proper Marriage*, but before *A Ripple from the Storm*. At the heart of this novel is a conflict between the world views of its two central characters. Julia Barr is an Eisenhower-years young woman, wanting only—or at least so she claims—to be left alone, to have a pleasant (but not too demanding) marriage and four well-spaced children, and not to be involved in the politics that have been so much a part of her parents' lives. Jan Brod, on the other hand, is a convinced Communist, even though he has been profoundly shaken by much that has gone on in his native Czechoslovakia, including the execution of his best friend (one can presume, although the novel is not specific, as part of something like the anti-Semitic Stalinist trials of Rudolf Slansky and his colleagues) and the red tape in the way of his own return to his homeland.

Several commentators have pointed out that Jan is the most fully convinced and the most appealing Communist in Lessing's fiction.[5] Like many others of her important male figures—Anton Hesse and Thomas Stern among them—Jan Brod is a European Jew, and, like Stern in relation to Martha, is vital, alive, charming, able to bring Julia to some understanding of his views, and, if not to a greater acceptance of politics, at least to a more personally liberated view of life. Jan goes to great pains to provide for Julia an understanding of his world view, to which Julia responds negatively with some heat and passion, although with a naiveté not usual in Lessing's women. Jan is thoughtfully concerned about the faults apparent to him in the Socialist world but persists, nonetheless, in the posture that "the Party is always right," because he is so fully committed to an understanding of the exploitation of poor people, of anti-Semitism, and of the horrors of fascism, as he has experienced them. He develops his world view with some degree of intellectual rigor, with poetic force, and with passion.

I see Jan's and Julia's story as a transitional one in Lessing's movement away from characters who are convinced Communists. It stands between the firm commitment to Communist ideology I have discussed in *A Proper Marriage* and Martha's disillusionment in first *A Ripple from the Storm* and, more fully, in *Landlocked* and later novels. By 1955, when, one can assume, *Retreat to Innocence* must have been at least in progress, some of the Stalinist violation of democracy and the executions, imprisonments, and other horrors which were part of Stalin's reign had impinged upon the consciousness of some Western Communists. By 1958, when *A Ripple from the Storm* was published, even the most convinced Western Communist party supporters had to accept the accuracy of these reported events, as Nikita Khrushchev revealed them and verified what had been rumor, at the famous twentieth congress of the Communist party of the Soviet Union. The result, for many European and American Communists, was devastating. Communist idols fell with a resounding smash as statues of Stalin fell in some Soviet and East European cities, defenses of Soviet harshness and lack of personal freedom proved impossibly hollow—and then the entire hagiography and pro-Soviet ideological defense structure came totally apart with the rumble of Soviet tanks in the streets of Budapest.

When Lessing prepared *A Ripple from the Storm* for publication, then, it is little wonder that she gave Martha Quest an outlook increasingly disillusioned with communism. Although Lessing had to work carefully so as not to violate the historicity of the mid-1940s setting of her novel, she nevertheless moves Martha and the Communist party group which is her "family" increasingly toward disarray and dissolution. I do not know, of course, if this development was entirely the result of post-1958 knowledge. However, if Lessing herself had long before then left earlier Communist commitments, at the very least the events of 1958 must have solidified her position. It is certainly worth noting that the earliest copyright dates cited for *Martha*

Quest and *A Proper Marriage* are 1952, while the earliest copyright dates cited for *A Ripple from the Storm* and *Landlocked* are 1958.

The very tone of Martha's world view in *A Ripple from the Storm*, as well as the political content of her life, contrast sharply with that of the earlier novels in *Children of Violence*. In *Martha Quest* and *A Proper Marriage* radical politics is a means, not only toward social change, but also toward personal freedom for Martha. In *A Ripple from the Storm* politics is a wearying, hopeless enterprise, shackling Martha in new ways, not terribly different from those in which she was earlier shackled by parents and the farm, "sundowners," marriage and child. Not only does the now very competent Martha run frantically but fruitlessly from meeting to meeting, but she also enters into an essentially political marriage, which turns out to be as empty and degrading as was her marriage to Douglas Knowell.

If Jan Brod is Lessing's most attractive Communist, then surely Anton Hesse is the least attractive, a grating, doctrinaire, dictatorial man without love or regard for others. Nothing could be more telling of the shift in these novels' points of view than that the convinced Leninist Hesse will, before the action in *Landlocked* is over, have accepted a middle-class wife—and a role in her father's business. Surely the most exciting "intellectual physiognomy" to come out of this novel is that of Thomas Stern, who stands in the sharpest possible contrast to Hesse. One way to see the shift in outlook I am discussing is to see *A Ripple from the Storm* and *Landlocked* as novels in which Martha's allegiances shift from the shopworn ideology of the Communist party and its arid brand of socialism, to Thomas Stern's intense, self-sacrificing, nearly mad desire to undo injustice—with a passion like Jan Brod's, but, although essentially socialist, without Brod's reliance on "the Party."

In *Landlocked* politics becomes, for all practical purposes, a secondary matter in Martha's life. She is still involved, but the dissolution of the party group, already foreshadowed in the previous novel, is completed in this one, and the most important of the Communist party members are either dead or out of action by the end of it—Anton Hesse married and in business; Athen, the Greek revolutionary who was something of an exemplary figure, probably killed by "the Colonels" in Greece; the English airmen gone back home to England. Even Thomas Stern, whose personal radicalism was so intense, dies in this novel, leaving Matty bereft and empty. All of Martha's political hopes, even her hopes that politics will provide a means of personal liberation for the women she has known, go glimmering. She describes her women Communist party friends: "In short they were all, already in their late twenties, early thirties, middle-aged women, neurotic with dissatisfaction, just as if they had never made resolutions not to succumb to the colonial small-town atmosphere."[6] The only character who seems to escape this fate is the vital and pragmatic Communist Jasmine Cohen, who, however, has left Zambesia to go to South Africa, where things seem clearer. [Feminist criticism, much more fully developed now than it was when these novels were published, would, I think, find interesting questions to ask about this description of the "women of the party," although again, those questions were not as yet on the "critical agenda," so to speak, when I first wrote this essay. That Jasmine Cohen, Thomas Stern, Jan Brod, and many others as well, often the "best" of her characters, are all Jewish raises an issue in Lessing's work which, in so far as I know, has not been sufficiently explored and which cannot be explored further here.]

Thus, *Landlocked* is the final step in a movement away from the Communist viewpoint held by many of the important characters in the first two novels of *Children of Violence*, a viewpoint aptly described by Maynard's comment—the Children of Violence are also the children of the French and Russian revolutions. It must be pointed out that in the last two novels of *Children of Violence*, or for that matter, in any Lessing novel, even those written much later, there are always characters who provide extensive critiques of the societies in which they live. Martha Quest and Thomas Stern, Jasmine Cohen, and others as well, continue to care deeply about the racism and exploitation they see about them. How the individual can respond fruitfully to such an awareness of injustice and inequality—that is what changes, and that is what is so different at the end of *Children of Violence*, as compared to the earlier novels in the quintet.

The Golden Notebook, in the political sense I am discussing here, is really part of the same period in Lessing's work as is *Landlocked*. Published in 1962, it is set in 1957—nearly a decade after *Landlocked*—during the period when the post-Khrushchev Communist world in the West was breaking up, and its subject matter is, in part, that breakup. It would take too much space here to detail the varieties of world views provided by *The Golden Notebook*, whether we consider the views of the fictional characters created by Anna Wulf, or those of the "real" characters in Anna's life. Suffice it to say that, although concern for alienation, for oppression, continue to be crucial aspects of this novel's themes, every kind of involvement in radical politics fails, from Anna's own Communist party activities to Tommy's feeble and disastrous pass at the "new left." Perhaps even more telling, especially in comparison to the earlier works in *Children of Violence*, the failure is a double failure—as a means for changing the social situation or as a means for providing satisfaction in the lives of the characters involved.

There is not, in this novel, any developed, articulate speaker for Communist political views—not even as unpleasant a person as Anton Hesse, certainly no one as sympathetic as Jan Brod, and certainly no one whose feelings about oppression, whose sense of justice and whose vitality is as powerful as Thomas Stern's. The men who surround Anna or Ella or Molly, are, by and large, neurotic ex-Communists, whose flirtations with radicalism ceased some time ago, who are now more likely to be in the office of the analyst than in the office of the party. There is no Jasmine Cohen either, no woman with the shrewd, articulate intelligence and radical dedication of that figure from *Children of Violence*.

Yet, quite obviously, *The Golden Notebook* is not an apolitical novel. If anything, it is Lessing's most manifestly political work, as the red notebook chronicles the breakdown of the British Communist party, and as Ella, in the fictionalized yellow notebook, grapples with her own relationship to the party. But Communism has surely failed completely here, either as a politics or a guide for living, and the problem of the novel is to find new guidelines for the lives of its radical "free women"

—who are free now in many ways, including their separation from, and thus freedom from, the demands of the party. Nothing could be more telling of the eventual world view of the novel's major characters than Anna's decision, announced to Molly at the end of the novel, that she will go to work in a marriage welfare center and that she will "join the Labour Party and teach night classes twice a week for delinquent kids." Although Anna doesn't much like her tone, Molly sums up the situation when she says: "So we're both going to be integrated with British life at its roots."[7]

In *The Four-Gated City*, one feels quite soon that radical politics, or really, all the earlier parts of Martha's life, have dropped to the periphery of the novel's concerns. Martha is, in fact, making a conscious effort to become, as it were, *tabula rasa* in England, as she looks for a new world view and a new role for herself. In a most cogent passage early in the novel, she decides that she must soon "cross the river" because she could not long continue as "a taste or flavour of existence without a name." In the next paragraph, Martha spends the afternoon and evening with a man to whom she identifies herself as "Phyllis Jones, with an imaginary history of war-time work in Bristol."[8]

As the novel progresses, it shifts radically the kind of world view Martha has. If the center of her earlier concerns was a Communist political one, the center of her concerns soon turns on Lynda Coldridge's psychic one. R.D. Laing, it seems to me, [in what has by now become a commonplace of Lessing criticism] has described the nature of Martha's and Lynda's efforts quite succinctly. He writes that

> the person who has entered this inner realm (if only he is allowed to experience this) will find himself going, or being conducted—one cannot clearly distinguish active from passive here—on a journey.
>
> This journey is experienced as going further "in," as going back through one's personal life, in and back and through and beyond into the experience of all mankind, of the primal man, of Adam and perhaps even further into the beings of animals, vegetables and minerals.[9]

Laing's views are certainly not, in any ordinary sense, apolitical. Laing, as well as Lessing in *The Four-Gated City* and subsequent work, looks for the solution to what conventional radical thought conceived of as systemic political problems in another dimension, in a kind of psychological—not to say psychic—expansion of consciousness. In the last sections of *The Four-Gated City*, which are essentially a form of science fiction [which has become so important a part of Lessing's more recent work], we see through Martha's new world view, the relevance of such concepts to political and social problems. Martha retains her concerns about the possibilities of nuclear cataclysm, the abuse of power, and racism, which have been familiar in her earlier world view. But the responses posed are not those having to do primarily with the restructuring of institutions or the redistribution of power—rather, they have to do with a new possible dimension for humankind. What we are given in this novel is the result of the failure of political solutions, failure so profound that it leads to some sort of unidentified worldwide catastrophe.

It seems to me that such an examination of the changes in world view of the characters in Lessing's novels can help us to understand her work in a number of ways. Here, I am interested in two problems, as I have said earlier. The first of these has to do with the changing form of their novels as Lessing's characters develop differing views of their experience.

The first four novels of *Children of Violence*, and *Retreat to Innocence*, I suggest, are essentially rather straightforward realistic novels, in the tradition of the "social" novel from, say, Samuel Richardson through the earlier work of Thomas Mann, or the fiction of C.P. Snow, with little of the experimentation with point of view, or time, so characteristic of so much of modern and postmodern fiction. The function of these novels is, precisely, to provide a picture of the "real," objective world and the way in which that world impinges upon the consciousness of the protagonists of the novels and of other important characters. Their point of view is consistently that of a third-person omniscient narrator, although the dominant consciousness of the works is, no doubt, that of Martha Quest. From time to time, an authorial voice is heard, commenting on the action. [In addition to whatever other reasons there may have been for Lessing's adoption of this form early in her work, it is also possible that she was working under the influence of Soviet-supported notions of "realism," notions which prevented even so brilliant a mind as Lukacs's from seeing the value or importance of many modern and postmodern writers.]

But in *The Four-Gated City* and *The Golden Notebook*, where the world view of the major characters has changed drastically, the form of the novels changes also. Thus, in *The Golden Notebook*, which is in one sense about the search for a new world view and the loss of an older one, the device of the notebooks permits Lessing quite a different focus than the focus of the earlier novels upon social reality and a character's conflict with that reality. The notebooks themselves provide us with a form of insight into the character's consciousness, including her consciousness as an artist, a writer, while other notebooks give us, respectively, political "history," Anna Wulf's created fiction which comments upon Anna's own experience, a form of the personal diary, and so on. The "Free Women" sections demonstrate in action the consequences in the "real life" of the novel of Anna's developing, changing, sometimes failing world view and the psychological states which—take your choice— either cause it or are caused by it. Thus, in *The Golden Notebook*, Lessing becomes a participant in the experimentation in novelistic form so common in our time, because she has abandoned the certainties of the world view which dominated at least *Martha Quest* and *A Proper Marriage*, and which continue to hold sway—albeit a much weakened sway—in *A Ripple from the Storm* and *Retreat to Innocence*, and which is really no longer a force, except in a negative sense in *Landlocked*. Lessing's form has changed, after these novels, then, as her characters' ideology—their world view—has changed.

The same comment, it seems to me, can be made about *The Four-Gated City*. In this novel, the change in form is not quite so drastic as in *The Golden Notebook*, because roughly the first half of the novel at least is cast in the form used throughout the other volumes in *Children of Violence*, although it is true that at some point in the middle of this book Lessing no longer gives the sharp, compassionate, and intriguing characterizations of her earlier work and creates what are by and large "flat" figures, meant to serve one or another exemplary purpose. But at the end of the novel, in part 4, when Martha is fully involved with Lynda Coldridge and the search for "mind expansion," the form changes quite drastically, until, in the "future" of the appendix, we get forms much closer to the science fiction novel than to the social novel. If *The Four-Gated City* is to some extent confused and fails to "work" as well as do the first four *Children of Violence* novels, that is, in part, I believe, because the new world view of the major characters has not as yet been cast in a form in which it can be most successfully expressed. [Lessing was to find the appropriate forms before too long, in such works as *Briefing for a Descent into Hell*, *Memoirs of a Survivor*, and *The Summer before the Dark*, and in the last of these especially in the penultimate section.]

The shift I have suggested raises another problem. The earlier novels under discussion here are certainly works that portray a radical ideology. But the *nature* of that radical ideology is, I think, of importance in understanding the shift in Lessing's fiction that takes place in the later novels. I suggest that the world view of Lessing's important left-wing characters is *not* in any full sense Marxist, although it is certainly radical. Anton Hesse reads Lenin but never Marx; he discusses the need for a party but never talks about the fundamental ideology which leads to Leninist conclusions about the need for a party. Martha Quest understands a good deal and tells us a good deal about the forms of oppression she sees in her society, but she rarely if ever discusses, say, the Marxist concept of alienation, which is really the underlying malaise she tries so desperately to escape. Even Jan Brod, the most sympathetic and most articulate and passionate of Lessing's Communists, discusses the need for struggle, talks movingly about fascism and anti-Semitism and about the need for the poor to take their destiny into their own hands, but he never discusses the basis of a Marxist view of human beings in society or of the relationship of the mode of production to the methods of production or the nature of commodity capitalism. [That none of Lessing's characters give voice to ideas articulated in the *Grundrisse*, that work of Marx's which has had perhaps the most profound effect on more recent Marxist thought, is not surprising, because that work's importance was not seen by any large group until after the novels under discussion here were written. One wonders what effect on the ideology of Lessing's characters might have resulted from such an awareness.]

The point I am trying to make here is a difficult one, and I make it only in a suggestive manner, because I find that I have no comparisons in fiction to which I can point for a positive example. As I think of the novelists in the recent past who have been avowedly Communists or Marxists, I find that none of them has really given us characters with a fully Marxist world view. To take only a few scattered examples, one thinks of André Malraux in *Man's Hope* or *Man's Fate*, of Haldor Laxness in *Independent People*, of the Soviet writer Ilya Ehrenburg in *The Storm*, or of John Dos Passos in *U.S.A.*—to find that what I have said here of Lessing's characters is true of theirs also. All these writers have written "radical" novels, in the tradition of the "bourgeois" novel, but none of them has given us characters whose world view is readily identifiable as Marxist.

If I seek for an example of what I mean by Marxist world view in literature I find that I must turn to Bertolt Brecht's theater, in that phase of his work that Darko Suvin has described as his "mature" phase. Suvin's description of an aspect of that phase will make my point clearer.

> Using the language of dialectical estrangement to master the alienated world, Brecht's mature aesthetic is not based on pure idea. It is in a permanent two-way relation of theory to practice, and may therefore be claimed as anti-ideological. . . . To man on the stage and the artistic representation of his relations to his fellow men, Brecht's mature aesthetic vision says at the same time "yes" and "no." It says "yes" to him as human potential,

> looking back at him from the vantage point of the future; from the same point, it says "no" to him as *homo duplex*, a cleftman of his specific perverted time.... They [the plays] were always strategies of dealienation, of a striving towards an integrated mankind, of man concerned with what Brecht called the greatest art—the art of living.[10]

No novelist I know of has written work that can be described in similar terms, nor in any other terms that provide for a genuinely Marxist world view, either for the novel as a whole or for its major characters. We can certainly recognize and cite examples of novels that portray Christian, or psychoanalytic, or other such views of the world; we can describe such fictions and enumerate their attributes. In so far as I know, no novel that could be called Marxist in the same sense exists, nor can its attributes be described and differentiated from the "bourgeois" novel in the way in which Brecht's theater can be separated from the "bourgeois" theater. [Innumerable questions come to mind as I re-read this section of my essay. Is it possible to provide *characters* with a Marxist world view? In my Brecht example, it is the *plays*, not the characters, that can be described this way. If I think of characters who have a clear world view of *any* kind, I find myself less certain than I once was that I can think of any in works of fiction which are not so purely didactic as to become artistically inferior or which are not purely allegorical. The most obvious example, which comes to my mind with great force, is, of course, *The Brothers Karamazov*—but then, how many Dostoevskys are there? Nevertheless, I think the point holds—Lessing's characters were not conceived with any firm, developed Marxist notion in mind but with rather a far more vaguely "liberal" one.]

Selma R. Burkom describes Lessing's basic point of view as "humanist," a designation with which one can readily concur, without necessarily agreeing with all of the specific comparisons Burkom makes between Lessing's and E.M. Forster's humanism. Lessing's concerns are for a more fully humane view of the possibilities for human beings. Such a view is not contradictory to radical views, which are also concerned with establishing more humane possibilities for human beings. In this sense, "radicals" and Communists and humanists are to be distinguished from one another only from the point of view of strategies leading to the establishment of such conditions. And it is precisely with such strategies that Lessing's radical characters are primarily concerned, in the earlier novels, and not with a different view of the very nature of human experience, which one might expect from characters who have a fully absorbed Marxist world view. By the writing of *The Golden Notebook*, Lessing had pretty much abandoned the strategies espoused by Communists and radical socialists in her earlier fiction, had even abandoned as hopeless the kind of radical humanism we get from Thomas Stern, had, in fact, turned toward quite a different source as a possible means for the achievement of her humanist aims. What must be seen clearly, it seems to me, is that Lessing's characters' most fundamental view of the human experience had not changed as much as one might suppose—having been "humanist" all along, rather than Marxist, the change is one in strategies, and not one involving a redefinition of the nature of human experience.

Lessing's commitment from the beginning of her work, it seems, was not to Marxist thought and its revolutionary components, but rather to radical humanist thought. What the world views of Lessing's most important characters demonstrate, then, is really a rather accurate picture of the world view of large sections of the movement she is describing. Never thoroughly Marxist, never fully conversant with Marx's most profound thought [and not yet aware of the impact of the *Grundrisse* on more recent Marxist thinking, or with the thought of Marx's most significant followers in our own time (one can cite Antonio Gramsci as exemplary here)], many radicals of the forties and fifties did indeed suffer disillusionment so profound that they searched for other, nonpolitical means for responding to a world their sensibilities continued to find disastrous. Some moved to hedonism, some to psychic restructuring, some to unassimilated Buddhism or the occult, and still others to an old-fashioned liberalism. Lessing's portrayal, then, of the development of Martha Quest's world view in *Children of Violence* is a possibly accurate portrayal of a real phenomenon in the Western world; her portrayal of Anna's search for a world view an example of the function of the social novel as it portrays the effect of idea and psychic state on the individual in his or her time.

This essay is not the appropriate place for discussion of the literary and nonliterary problems such a reading of Lessing raises—would the breakup of the Left have been less traumatic in Western countries had there been fuller understanding of Marxism; was it in part a result of blindly following the Soviet model which led Western Communists to such despair; in what way, if any, does Leninism, as distinguished from Marxism, play a role in preventing full access for Westerners to Marxist thought; what would a Marxist novel look like, and is such a novel a possibility—and other such questions. [Was Lessing reflecting, in her early fiction, a crisis in Marxism in general which, in the last decade or so, has assumed enormous proportions, informed by rereadings of Marx, further splintering of the British and American Left, sharp divisions within the world's Marxist states, failures of the ostensible predictive powers of Marxist analysis? What effect on Lukacs's dictum have poststructuralist critical concepts had, for example, given the questioning of the relationship between literature and some—if any—knowable reality, is the requirement that literary characters display a *Weltanschauung* still sustainable, and what does that requirement mean?]

It is to be hoped, however, that this charting of the role of world view in Lessing's fiction does help us to see her as a novelist who is rather whole, moving us from one to another "bourgeois radical" (I will ask to be forgiven the cant phrase, for brevity's sake) point of view with relative ease, and in the process writing a fiction that accurately portrays an aspect of our social experience. It helps us, I believe, to see her as a novelist in the tradition of the realistic social novel, even when the changes in her characters' world views lead into experimentation with form to suit these newer views. It helps us, finally, to see Lessing as a novelist whose characters' ideology is consistent at least to the extent that they are always concerned with injustice, with human degradation—whether as Communists, as women seeking freedom from sexist oppression, or as searchers for the "inner space"—and with the means for changing the world.

NOTES

1. Georg Lukacs, "The Intellectual Physiognomy of Literary Characters," trans. L.E. Mins, in *Radical Perspectives in The Arts*, ed. Lee Baxandall (Harmondsworth, Middlesex, England: Penguin Books, 1972), 90.

2. I have enclosed in square brackets comments which are not part of the original paper presented here but which seem to me necessary as a result of rereading, some thirteen years after the paper was first written. In the rest of the paper, the only changes made are those that have to do with minor emendations of style or with changes necessitated by converting to written form a work first presented orally.

3. I am considering here only fiction by Lessing up to and including *The Four-Gated City* because the particular development in which I am interested is substantially accomplished by the end of the novel. For the sake of simplicity, I do not deal with other work written by Lessing prior to 1965, such as *The Grass Is Singing*, her short fiction, her plays, or such hybrid forms as *In Pursuit of the English*. Although all these works are certainly deserving of comment, nothing in them adds to or substantially changes my thesis.

4. Doris Lessing, *A Proper Marriage* (New York: American Library Plume Books, 1970), 345.

5. Noel Elizabeth Alcorn, "Vision and Nightmare: A Study of Doris Lessing's Novels" (Ph.D. Diss., University of California at Irvine, 1971), 1.

6. Doris Lessing, *Landlocked* (New York: American Library Plume Books, 1970), 205.

7. Doris Lessing, *The Golden Notebook* (New York: Ballantine, 1972), 665-66.

8. Doris Lessing, *The Four-Gated City* (London: MacGibbon & Kee, 1969), 29.

9. R.D. Laing, "The Schizophrenic Experience," in *The Politics of Experience* (New York: Ballantine, 1972), 126. Laing points out in his acknowledgments that earlier versions of this essay appeared in several different places in 1964. For further comment concerning Laing and Lessing, see especially Paul Schlueter, *The Novels of Doris Lessing* (Carbondale, Southern Illinois Press, 1973), p. 123 n. 5, et passim.

10. Darko Suvin, "The Mirror and the Dynamo," in *Radical Perspectives In The Arts*, 87-88.

MOLLY HITE

Subverting the Ideology of Coherence: *The Golden Notebook* and *The Four-Gated City*

"THE POINT IS," INSISTS ANNA AT THE OPENING OF *The Golden Notebook* "the point is, that as far as I can see, everything's cracking up."[1] It is a point that the novel goes on to consider at some length, most evidently in its treatment of the failure of a single world view to encompass the whole of twentieth-century reality. Both Anna and her creator have a particular world view in mind, of course, the orthodox Marxism of the mid-1950s that is so thoroughly repudiated as Anna herself moves toward and beyond "crack-up." But the critique of Marxist ideology begun in *The Golden Notebook* also goes much further, addressing the assumption that any world view can be adequate, that reality is the sort of thing that can be held together as a unified whole. This assumption was what Lessing found most congenial in Marxist aesthetics and upheld in her 1957 essay "The Small Personal Voice," where she made unity of vision the hallmark of the novels she termed "the highest point of literature," the classics of nineteenth-century realism. In this essay, realism is identified with both metaphysical and moral coherence—the great writers of the period produced "art which springs so vigorously and naturally from a strongly-held, though not necessarily intellectually-defined, view of life that it absorbs symbolism" and had in common "a climate of ethical judgement; they shared certain values; they were humanists."[2]

But the tone throughout the essay is nostalgic, and the emphasis on coherence is in fact the party line for the period.[3] In *The Golden Notebook*, Lessing dissects and dismisses the appeal of both nostalgia and party. And despite the rhetoric of wholeness that informs both this novel and the subsequent book with which it is most frequently compared, *The Four-Gated City*, her theory of fiction changes radically after "The Small Personal Voice," so that these two encyclopedic novels function as transitional works marking her turn away from realist conventions and especially the convention of coherence, which like all conventions emerges as at root an ideological construct. Although *The Golden Notebook* and *The Four-Gated City* are indubitably *about* coherence, neither is by realist conventions coherent. And in both, Lessing subjects the convention of coherence, along with its ideological underpinnings, to close scrutiny.

In *The Golden Notebook* she is most obviously examining the coherence expected of characters in realistic fiction, the assumptions behind the notion of identity; as when Anna opposes people who are "cracked across" or "split," or the man with "a crack in [his] personality like a gap in a dam, and through that gap the future might pour in a different shape," to the catalog of Jungian archetypes that, according to her politically named psychoanalyst Mrs. Marks, exhaust the forms of human possibility (p. 473). Such "cracks" and "gaps" imply at least the possibility of something utterly new and thus wholly outside traditional modes of representation. Similarly, she suggests that the thematic and structural coherence of the traditional novel is evidence less of "a climate of ethical judgement" than of a limitation more damaging in that it is not perceived. By systematically subverting the form of the traditional novel, she subverts the assumption that this form is the natural structure of all possible experience.

"The game" that Anna plays in *The Golden Notebook* is one analogue of this form and implicitly parodies conventional notions of novelistic coherence. Something like a meditative exercise, "the game" seems initially to be a means of expanding consciousness and overcoming fragmentation, in which the player "creates" in her imagination her immediate surroundings and then progressively enlarges her scope to comprehend the entire universe, the ultimate purpose being to achieve "a simultaneous knowledge of vastness and of smallness" (p. 548). But the kind of knowledge that Anna aims for, in effect the omniscience of the nineteenth-century narrator, is finally insufficient because it presumes a fixed, "outside" location for the "creator" that allows her to remain both detached and in control (significantly, Anna envisions herself *above* the spinning globe her imagination encompasses). Knowledge of this sort assumes that there is a position of observation, and thus an angle of vision, that is the "correct" one and in this way imposes a particular form: the thing known, like the character labeled with the name of a Jungian archetype, is contained, distanced, fixed. Anna's published novel, *Frontiers of War,* resulted from her having made a set of events in her past into a "story"—a product of hindsight, a reviewing of experience *sub specie resolutionis*—and her attitude of "lying nostalgia" toward these events is a yearning for the apparent stasis and finish of a closed-off past comprehended completely. It is only at the climax of her breakdown, when she finds viewing "conventionally well-made films" that parody the conventions she herself has taken for granted in imaging this part of her life, that Anna realizes how limited her vision has been. " 'And what makes you think the emphasis you have put on it is the correct emphasis?' " inquires the projectionist who plays ironic Virgil to her Dante in this dream vision, and she notes the paradoxically Marxist use of the word *correct* throwing finally into question the notion of a coherent single world view arising from a privileged viewpoint (p. 618). "Literature is analysis after the event," she had written much earlier (p. 228), and much of the experience she undergoes in this novel has been forcing on her the conclusion that literature, as she has always understood it, invariably falsifies by refusing to acknowledge that "after the event" is only one perspective. But now the projectionist presses further. " 'How would June Boothby see that time? I bet you can't do June Boothby,' " he says (p. 619), suddenly foregrounding someone who in Anna's memory—and in *The Golden Notebook*—functions as a minor character. The irresistible implication is that every perspective is as "correct" as every other perspective, that the whole, if such a thing is even conceivable, is constituted by all possible perspectives, and therefore that an apprehension of the whole is, strictly speaking, impossible.

The structure of the novel reinforces this conclusion, parodying and ultimately subverting the desire for a comprehensive vision. Like much truly radical literature, *The Golden Notebook* has been widely read as if it were a traditional realist novel with a few experimental twists, at root cohering as a single story that can be resolved into levels of framing. But the hierarchy of levels is unstable, as if in response to the projectionist's question "And what make you think the emphasis you have put on it is the correct emphasis?" and there are several occasions when the naturalizing device of levels simply fails to organize the material. The apparent containing fiction, "Free Women," not only becomes less important as the novel progresses, but it also begins to diverge from the notebooks in matters of plot, particularly in the stories of Tommy, who in "Free Women" shoots and blinds himself but in the blue notebook only grows up in a predictably irritating way, and of Anna's affair with the American—the pivotal experience with Saul Green in the blue notebook, a much more condensed and less extreme relationship with a man named Milt in "Free Women." Furthermore, "Free Women" and the notebooks tell stories with different and irreconcilable endings. In "Free Women" the discourse essentially returns to its starting point: the two women who began the story alone in the London flat now kiss and separate, each going off to attend to her own compromised ideals, and Molly's shorthand tag, "It's all very odd, isn't it Anna?" sums up the preceding action and confirms that the dry, ironic tone Anna was trying to elude in the opening scene has triumphed. The notebooks, on the other hand, have a wholly different "ending," in which Anna, prompted by Saul Green, writes a novel that could either be "Free Women"—in which case, as Lorna Sage acutely observes, "Lessing has produced what geometricians would call an impossible object, for the 'inner' space of the notebooks also contains its outer envelope"[4]—or *The Golden Notebook* itself, in which case the hitherto linear narrative reveals itself to be a Möbius strip. Furthermore, the distinction between ontological levels

—between fact and fiction within the narrative—is also blurred, as in the "merging" of Anna's Michael and Ella's Paul Tanner (pp. 616-17), or in Saul's comment implying that Anna and Molly are "really" aspects of a single person: " 'There are *the two women you are, Anna.* Write down: The two women were alone in the London flat' " (p. 639, emphasis added.)

In all these ways *The Golden Notebook* disperses both character and plot, challenging the claim of a single, holistic vision to contain ultimate truth. If this dispersal initially seems at odds with the novel's attack on compartmentalization, it eventually begins to expose conventional notions of unity as the most dangerous compartments of all because they do not acknowledge other possibilities. But Lessing's treatment of possibility in this novel is essentially negative; she is concerned to create the conditions that would allow the future to make an appearance but does little to indicate what shape it might take. Her emphasis is on the gaps and cracks. It is in *The Four-Gated City* that she makes the turn toward imaging possibility in positive ways.

In a sense, her method of doing this is disconcertingly literal-minded. It is precisely the future—that is, a chronological period situated after the time of writing—that is represented in *The Four-Gated City*, and it does not "pour in" so much as constitute a rather traditional conclusion, which fulfills and to an extent explains the premonitions of catastrophe and transformation informing earlier parts of the story. There are no containing or overlapping frames, no ambiguities arising from the testimony of multiple narrators, no grounds for confusion over which version of the story is the "correct" one.

But the representation of possibility in *The Four-Gated City* violates a somewhat different convention by mixing genres, introducing elements of what Lessing purposely calls by the trivializing name of "space fiction" and thus provoking a critical response anticipated by the book itself in discussions of the "distaste factor." Just as Anna in the course of Mrs. Mark's therapy attached names of archetypes to people in order to define them so completely they were incapable of surprising, Martha comes to recognize a social reflex prompting her to label certain ideas as "dotty," "eccentric," "shady," and so on (pp. 488-89),[5] epithets that can be, and to a certain extent have been, applied to *The Four-Gated City* itself. These labels, Martha realizes, generally work to contain the unfamiliar so that it can be dismissed, ruling out possibility and preventing the future from pouring through in a different shape. In *The Four-Gated City* Lessing has not, as in *The Golden Notebook*, tried to represent possibility in a new kind of writing. Rather, she has chosen to write an apparently traditional work that has imbedded in it instructions for a new kind of reading, one that refuses to rest in the apparent comprehensiveness and coherence of received opinion. The passages analyzing the "distaste factor" encourage the reader to recognize, examine, and resist conditioned responses to certain themes, most radically perhaps in the case of that monolithic concept "humanity," which the book suggests may be the most delusive ideological construct of all. One of Martha's key insights is that there is no intrinsic reason for assuming that human concerns have priority. Once she abandons this assumption, the notion of an essential humanity deconstructs itself, and human beings are exposed as "essentially isolated, shut in, enclosed inside their hideously defective bodies, behind their dreaming drugged eyes, above all, inside a net of wants and needs that made it impossible for them to think of anything else" (p. 481). No longer blinkered by societal preconceptions about the beauty and value of human being, Martha perceives the extent of human deficiency and isolation. Paradoxically, it is only by relinquishing the ideology of humanism that she can begin to understand the human condition.

Lessing also attempts to guide reading by proposing allegorical or typological models of interpretation in passages that must themselves be read allegorically or typologically. For instance, Martha and Lynda "used their dreams, their slips of the tongue, their fantasies . . . as maps or signposts for a country which lay just beyond or alongside, or within the landscape they could see and touch" (p. 355) but could not apprehend this new terrain directly: "It was as if the far-off sweetness experienced in a dream, that unearthly impossible sweetness, less the thing itself than the need or hunger for it . . . had come closer . . ." (p. 357). Although this nuanced and gestural language is similar to the language used in *The Golden Notebook* to describe the experience of breakdown, Lessing goes further in her later book, asserting a concept of human being that suggests why such passages do, in fact, communicate. If Anna rejected the Jungian doctrine of archetypes because it contradicted the potential in people for real novelty that was a fact of her experience, Martha appears to accept something like the Jungian doctrine of the collective unconscious because it confirms a fact of her experience: "If she was feeling something, in this particular way, with the authenticity, the irresistibility, of the growing point, then she was not alone, others were feeling the same . . ." (p. 485). Finally it is the mind itself that is universal. "It is not a question of 'Lynda's mind' or 'Martha's mind'; it is the human mind, or part of it, and Lynda, Martha, can choose to plug in or not" (p. 473). This idea is not simply a theme treated within the novel; it becomes a structural principle, ultimately destroying the coherence traditionally accorded to character. As she explores the implication of "plugging in," Martha, who for four volumes of the *Children of Violence* series has been a more or less conventional protagonist, dissolves into a series of roles, a vehicle for impersonal forces, one perspective in or version of a reality approached from other directions by other characters, to the point where her personal existence is so unimportant that her death is mentioned only in passing (p. 609). The effect of this diffusing of personality is to transform what had appeared to be a five-volume *Bildungsroman* into an experimental narrative that culminates in a repudiation of the ideology underlying theories of character and plot that makes the *Bildungsroman* possible. Lessing finally rejects realism by rejecting humanism.

One final qualification that takes us beyond the two novels under discussion: Or she rejects humanism inasmuch as she rejects realism. This qualification follows, of course, from Lessing's announcement in September 1984 that under the name of Jane Somers she wrote and published two recent novels, *The Diary of a Good Neighbour* and *If the Old Could. . . .* If the tendency of the books after *The Four-Gated City* has been to place human issues in a more and more cosmic context, with identifiably human characters disappearing entirely after

Shikasta, the Somers novels might appear to be reversions or even regressions to the comfortable assumptions and limits of traditional realism, in that both make the personal experience of human beings living in London in the immediate past their central concern and present a succession of events leading up to a climax and denouement through an unproblematic first-person narrator. *Newsweek* greeted them with relief as "straightforward storytelling,"[6] and certainly there are no intrusive "cracks" or "gaps" within these stories that call attention to, and thus help subvert, the conventions of writing or of reading. But the circumstances of their production involved violating another convention of coherence, introducing a "crack" or "gap" in the author herself. By Lessing's own testimony the split was necessary to allow something new to enter her work—the future in still another shape. In the preface to *Shikasta* she wrote of "the exhilaration that comes from being set free into a large scope, with more capacious possibilities and themes,"[7] and in her preface to the Vintage edition of the Jane Somers novels she describes a different kind of being set free, by implication at least as exhilarating. "As Jane Somers I wrote in ways that Doris Lessing cannot. . . . Jane Somers knew nothing about a kind of dryness, like a conscience, that monitors Doris Lessing whatever she writes and in whatever style."[8] Perhaps one reason Jane Somers "knows nothing" about this dryness, which readers, too, associate with Doris Lessing, is that as narrator-protagonist Somers has been carefully conceived as someone who knows nothing about the Marxist world view, which Lessing has been compelled to acknowledge, if not embrace, in virtually all her previous work, and thus is free to *discover* the penury, humiliations, and unexpected appeal of the very old whom she takes as her subject matter, without subordinating these phenomena to a preexisting framework of class analysis. At any rate, this testimony implies that Lessing has found the assumption of authorial coherence at least as constricting—and at least as arbitrary—as the realist conventions requiring characters to be self-consistent, individual, and identifiable. Once again, some sort of violation of coherence was necessary to create a space for possibility.

Notes

1. Doris Lessing, *The Golden Notebook* (New York: Bantam, 1981) All references are to this edition; subsequent page references appear in parentheses in the text.

2. Doris Lessing, In *A Small Personal Voice: Essays, Reviews, Interviews*, ed. Paul Schlueter (New York: Vintage, 1974), 4-5.

3. For instance, a more doctrinaire critic of the period, Jack Lindsay, calls upon contemporary novelists to return to a "consciousness of unity of process which is adequate to deal with all aspects of life, social, artistic, scientific, yet see each separate aspect in relation to the whole." See Lindsay, *After The Thirties* (London: Lawrence & Wishart, 1956), 34, quoted in Jenny Taylor's "Introduction: Situating Reading," in *Notebooks/Memoirs/Archives: Reading and Rereading Doris Lessing* (Boston: Routledge & Kegan Paul, 1982), 29. Taylor's introduction contains an informative account of Lessing's relation to the English Left in the 1950s, as does Lorna Sage's *Doris Lessing* (London and New York: Methuen Contemporary Writers Series, 1983), esp. 43-49.

4. Sage, 55. Sage's study is the most far-reaching examination to date of the implications of Lessing's deconstructed—or, to borrow Sage's evocative metaphor, decolonized—narratives.

5. Doris Lessing, *The Four-Gated City* (New York: Alfred A. Knopf, 1969). All references are to this edition; subsequent page references appear in parentheses in the text.

6. "What's in a Literary Name," Walter Clemons, with Donna Foote and Ray Sawhill, *Newsweek* 1 Oct. 1984, 89.

7. Doris Lessing, *Re: Colonized Planet 5: Shikasta* (New York: Alfred A. Knopf, 1979), ix.

8. Doris Lessing, *The Diaries of Jane Somers* (New York: Vintage, 1984), viii.

Alvin Sullivan

Ideology and Form: Decentrism in *The Golden Notebook, Memoirs of a Survivor*, and *Shikasta*

One of the self-evident features of Doris Lessing's work is an abrupt change of form, beginning with *The Golden Notebook*. This pattern holds for such later works as *The Memoirs of a Survivor, Shikasta,* and *The Marriages of Zones Three, Four, and Five.*

As readers, we attempt to order a work, spatially or in other ways, when it appears to have no order or none that is familiar from earlier works. We are conditioned to see a literary work as a totality or unity—either a constructed totality or an organic one. We believe traditionally in a unity of form and content, both supplying an ideology. One Marxist critic, however, rejects that belief. Pierre Macherey asserts that

> a work is tied to ideology not so much by what it says as what it does not say. It is in the significant *silences* of a text, in its gaps and advances that the presence of ideology can be most positively felt. . . . In trying to tell the truth in his own way, for example, the author finds himself forced to reveal the limits of the ideology within which he writes.[1]

As long as a text contains gaps or "silences" it is always incomplete and not unified. Instead of a coherent whole, it is a contradiction of meanings. There is no central structure; the work is always "decentered," "dispersed," "diverse," "irregular" (all Macherey's terms). The reader's or critic's task is not to impose patterns—the Hegelian-structuralist activity of reconstituting an object—nor to "fill in" the gaps. Instead, "we should question the work as to what it does not and cannot say, in those silences for which it has been made. . . . The disorder that permeates the work is related to the disorder of ideology. . . ."[2]

Although Macherey's concern is author-based, he agrees with reader-based phenomenologists like Umberto Eco and Wolfgang Iser that form is a determinate constituent. What Macherey hails as a decentered text, Eco refers to as a *metaphor epistemologique,* a fragmentary form that reflects the way in which contemporary culture views reality. We are not required to put fragments together but to recognize that the meaning is a "picture of fragments." Similarly, Iser allows only a "configurative meaning" for texts: a "*pars pro toto* fulfillment."[3] Both would agree with Macherey that "it is impossible for a specific work to reproduce the totality of an ideology: a partial apprehension is all that is possible. . . . Ideology is not, prior to the work, like a system which can be reproduced; it is resumed, elaborated by the work. . . .[4]

Lessing's introduction to a reprinting of *The Golden Notebook*, ten years after its first publication, suggests her critical affinity with Macherey, Eco, Iser. "The book is alive and potent and fructifying and able to promote thought and discussion *only* when its plan and shape and intention are not understood. . . ." The form of the novel was to be its own ideology, and that "a wordless statement"; it would "talk through the way it was shaped."[5] It remains for us to ask not, "What shape does the book have?" but why the work assumes a particular shape. In Macherey's terms: "The work exists on the reverse side (*envers*) of what it would like to be, the reverse of itself. Where is this reverse?"[6] It is a question we might briefly explore for *The Golden Notebook*, noting its importance also for two later works, *The Memoirs of a Survivor* and *Shikasta.*

Of the three, only the form of *Memoirs* appears to be conventional. *The Golden Notebook* uses six distinct modes in the four notebooks, the "later" golden notebook, and the "Free Women" envelope. The notebooks are ordered by topic or approach: the fuzzy personal recollections (memoirs) of the black notebook, the introduction of historical events in the red, the fictionalized treatment of the yellow, the factual reporting of the blue. Ultimately, the black deteriorates narratively to a collage of clippings, and two notebooks are abandoned. Narrators become characters become narrators: Lessing writes about Anna Wulf writing about Ella. Fictionalized characters have their more-or-less fictionalized counterparts: Willi is Max, Paul is Michael. A fictional character invents a fictional alter ego: a fictional Saul with qualities of a "real" Milt arrives to replace a "real" Janet. Together, Saul and Anna create the golden notebook, and Saul begins Anna's novel while Anna writes Saul Green's short story. Against this level of conscious experience are juxtaposed dream sequences, wherein characters are symbolized or mythologized, and a film is presumably "projected" by Saul.

Undeniably, there are patterns to be discovered here, structures to be explained, relationships to be explored. In the act of describing the form of the novel, I have already necessarily "interpreted" it in one or more ways. The success of the novel owes to the discoveries the reader is forced to make for himself or herself by the silences of the text. As Iser reminds us, we "only conduct these 'interpretative acts' " when "the system of presentation leaves out the coordinating elements between observable phenomena and situations."[7] To pursue connections in order to construct a "reality" for the work is both necessary and pointless—necessary to establish a meaning, pointless because whatever meaning we decide the work has will never "explain" the work.

Instead, if Macherey is right, the form that the novel has taken will tell us the form it was unable to assume. We recognize two kinds of writing in *The Golden Notebook*: the raw data and sketches of the notebooks, the finished genre of "Free Women." From our reading we select any number of plots, one of which is that Anna is unable to write. In the first blue notebook entries, where Anna recounts her psychoanalysis, she maintains, "I'm not here because I'm suffering from a writer's block" (p. 232). But the action of the novel builds to the end of the blue notebook, to the moment when she is able to admit to Saul that she has a block, and to the dreams recounted in the golden notebook that free her to write. (Concomitant with Anna's discovery is that of the reader; not until the golden notebook is he or she aware that the "Free Women" sections are also Anna's fictions.) Thus one theme of the novel: that the conscious production of a literary work, the expression of reality in one specific, generic structure, is impossible.

To be sure, the novel is as much about Anna's illness, her sexual dysfunction, or the pursuit of truth. But all these subjects are inextricably linked to her writing. In this way the novel is actually decentered in relation to what seems to be its essential preoccupation, the struggle for identity that Anna undergoes. All her needs are projected onto her fictions. The first plot summary that Anna writes is a recognition of the reality of her situation, her invention of Saul. "A woman, starved for love, meets a man rather younger than herself, younger perhaps in emotional experience. . . . She deludes herself about the nature of the man; for him, another love affair merely" (p. 531). As she recognizes that all her projections are herself—"I've been the malicious old man, and the spiteful old woman, or both together" (p. 563)—she no longer needs four notebooks: "it's been necessary to split myself up, but from now on I shall be using one only" (p. 598). The discoveries about herself she transfers to her writing. She first differentiates "what I had invented and what I had known, and I knew that what I had invented was all false" (pp. 619-20). At the end she decides that all writing is false. "The fact is, the real experience can't be described. I think, bitterly, that a row of asterisks, like an old-fashioned novel, might be better. . . . Anything at all, but not words" (p. 633).

If we agree that Anna is a typification, a character who "concentrates and intensifies a much more general reality,"[8] we proceed to examine how that reality is differentiated. Historically, we have classified treatments of artists or the development of artistic consciousness as *Kunstlerromans*. *The Golden Notebook* fits a tradition including *The Sorrows of Young Werther*, for example, or *A Portrait of the Artist as a Young Man*. With Joyce's novel it shares several features and discusses common concerns: the self-preoccupations of the narrators, the arbitrariness of form and reality, the function of artists in society, the relation of artistic production to history, in sum, "the activity of the human spirit through which, in which, life continually seeks to understand itself, and, understanding, to re-create."[9]

Using *A Portrait* as a homology for *The Golden Notebook* has the effect of differentiation rather than correspondence. And nowhere is that differentiation more radical than in form. Joyce did not choose *A Portrait* to be an envelope (analogous to "Free Women") for *Stephen Hero*, his diary, and companion fiction (analogous to the four notebooks). We may rightly ask how differences in forms within one genre of discourse are accountable and resort to historical explanation.[10] Or we may cite textual evidence to indicate ideological differences. In Joyce's novel, for example, Stephen Dedalus prefers to see roses as green; it is his prerogative as artist to distort reality. Anna Wulf takes no such prerogative. It is her task to capture reality; her identity depends on the reality of words: "For words are form, and if I am at a pitch where shape, form, expression are nothing, then I am nothing" (p. 477). It is, however, too distorting of the text to extrapolate from such singular instances, as formalist criticism has done.

If we pose Macherey's question, what is the reverse side of the work? What would *The Golden Notebook* like to be? the answer is not, Joyce's novel. An analogous "finished work" is there —"Free Women"—and it is the least interesting part of the novel. There is more reality in the "raw" data of unfinished diaries, news clippings, dreams, film sequences, psychoanalysis. What is lacking is any external form that *can* subsume all these, in the way embryonic growth orders the development of *A Portrait* or mythic correspondences unify *Ulysses*. Each form in *The Golden Notebook* is as real or unreal as the next; each remains unconnected. The fictions of Anna Wulf "break" ideology, to use Macherey's term, rather than reflect it in some classical sense. The various forms build a determinate image of the ideological, revealing it as an object rather than living it from within "as though it were an inner consciousness." The function of literature is to demystify, not to be demystified; "because it naturally scorns the credulous view of the world," literature establishes illusion as a visible object.[11] Content and form, to use another critical focus, collaborate, not to produce a false unity but to break false consciousness. Anna Wulf discovers the relationship between reality and illusion, the falsity of the forms that must contain her experiences.

What is significant in Lessing's work after *The Golden Notebook* is the freedom from conventional generic forms, as evidence that the writing of this one novel was a liberating discovery. The realizations that illusions can demystify, that conventional realistic forms produce false consciousness, that decentering scatters the meaning of texts, all carry on. *The Memoirs of a Survivor* consistently uses illusion as if it is reality. The world beyond the wall of the narrator's flat is, presumably, the past that becomes the future. The imaginary is the real; the future is the present. But *Memoirs* uses a traditional symbol as a metalinguistic sign, as if Lessing were taking the advice of Anna Wulf: "real experience can't be described . . . a row of asterisks . . . might be better. Or a symbol of some kind, a circle, perhaps, or a square" (p. 633). In *Memoirs* the symbol is the yellow spot on the wall that permits entrance into the world beyond; it becomes increasingly identified with the cosmic egg whose shell is the world frame of space.[12] Even more than *The Golden Notebook*, *Memoirs* speaks through the complex oppositions that structure it. It manifests or uncovers what it cannot say. At the moment of the anticipated explanation, or closure, the narrator reports, "All I can say is, nothing at all." The meaning is the silence. It is not, Macherey avers, "a lack to be remedied." Rather, "this silence gives [the work] life."[13]

Shikasta heralds still another development in experimental forms. In its structures of conventional linear narratives, reports, early histories, journal entries, even fictional bibliographies, and its multiple narrators, *Shikasta* recalls *The Golden Notebook*. But the debate is no longer between fact and fiction, illusion and reality, madness and sanity, or memory and experience. The task of *Canopus in Argos*, or its "preintention," seems to be nothing less than providing apocalyptic posthuman history from the viewpoints of gods, devils, and whatever else may perch on a new great chain of being. Generically, the series promises to be allegory and fable, which it combines and reshapes. But the oracular tone of *Shikasta* is transmuted in *The Marriages of Zones Three, Four, and Five* to a romantic narrative, in much the same fashion as the historical, "outer-directed" red notebook of *The Golden Notebook* gives way to the personal fictions of the yellow.

The conditions that determine the production of *Canopus* will also determine the forms it will take to communicate. "From what new center is the work of fiction carried out?" Macherey asks. "It is not a question of a real center, for the book does not replace ideologically decentered illusion with a permanent center around which the system of language is to be ordered."[14] At this point in *Canopus* all that is clear is that we are being given, generically, science fiction as history: this is the frame Lessing seeks to fill. At the beginning we must admit the "impossibility of the work's filling the ideological frame for which it should have been made,"[15] but we wait nevertheless to see which themes will be developed, which images kept or discarded, and which forms emerge from the disparity between frame and subject. We wait, as Macherey would put it, to see what intervention the author will make in the production of the text. As readers, we proceed from an authorial directive, a titular clue: "archives": raw data, random residue, what was worth saving, or what merely survived. The gaps and silences of *Shikasta* are already inviting us to write future history, even as the succeeding volumes, author's interventions, will no doubt demand we revise.

Notes

1. Pierre Macherey, as summarized by Terry Eagleton, in *Marxism and Literary Criticism* (Berkeley: University of California Press, 1976), 34-35.

2. Macherey, *A Theory of Literary Production*, trans. Geoffrey Wall (London: Routledge & Kegan Paul, 1978), p. 155.

3. See Umberto Eco, *The Role of the Reader: Exploration in the Semiotics of the Text* (Bloomington: Indiana University Press, 1979), Chap. 1: "The Poetics of the Open Work." A better discussion of the *opera aperta* is his essay, *Opera aperta* (Milan, Italy: Bompiani, 1962). For a discussion in English of this essay, see Oscar Kenshur, "Fragments and Order," forthcoming in *Papers on Language and Literature*. See also, Wolfgang Iser, *The Implied Reader: Patterns of Communication in Prose Fiction from Bunyan to Beckett* (Baltimore: Johns Hopkins University Press, 1974), 285.

4. Macherey, *Theory of Literary Production*, 232.

5. Doris Lessing, *The Golden Notebook* (New York: Bantam, 1973), xxii. All references are to this edition; subsequent page references appear in parentheses in the text.

6. Macherey, *Theory of Literary Production*, 232.

7. Iser, *Implied Reader*, 204.

8. See Raymond Williams, *Marxism and Literature* (Oxford: Oxford University Press, 1977), 101-107.

9. S.L. Goldberg, *The Classical Temper* (London: Chatto & Windus, 1961), 262.

10. We may, for example, attribute the forms Joyce chooses to such contemporary philosophy as Bradley's ideas about the nature of reality or Wittgenstein's about language; critics have traced Lessing's sources in Sufism, for example. But, as Macherey emphasizes, the contradictions in a text "cannot be the same . . as those contradictions upon which the work depends, even if we should discover those same contradictions in the life of the artist" (See his *Theory of Literary*

Production, 232). See also Patrick Gardiner, *The Nature of Historical Explanation* (London: Oxford University Press, 1952), esp. 46-51, 119-20.

11. Macherey, *Theory of Literary Production*, 132-33.

12. See Sullivan, "Lessing's Notes toward a Supreme Fiction," *Modern Fiction Studies* 26 (1980): 160-61.

13. Macherey, *Theory of Literary Production*, 84.

14. Ibid., 64.

15. Ibid., 198.

KATHERINE FISHBURN

Teaching Doris Lessing as a Subversive Activity: A Response to the Preface to *The Golden Notebook*

EVER SINCE 1971, WHEN DORIS LESSING PUBLISHED THE preface to *The Golden Notebook* (1962), those of us who teach this novel have found ourselves in an untenable position vis à vis its author. Our position has been untenable because, in teaching *The Golden Notebook*, we seem to be contravening Lessing's express desire that her readers have direct and immediate access to her novel without critical or pedagogic interference. In this time, we have also found ourselves in an awkward position vis à vis our students, because Lessing, in her preface, advises them to ignore our opinions and experience the novel on their own terms. She gives this advice because she clearly worries that we will impose an interpretation, a reading of her novel, on our students—her readers. In effect, she is afraid that we will tell students what her novel means. This sort of didactic approach is anathema to Lessing because it denies the essence of what she is trying to do in her fiction. That is, by telling students what her book means, we would be denying them the dialectic exchange of ideas that Lessing intends them to experience for themselves as they read the text.

It seems to me that Lessing, by expressing these fears, has directed an open challenge to her critics and to those who would teach her fiction. What she has challenged us to do is come up with a way of criticizing and teaching her fiction that complements—if not forwards—her own purpose in writing. The questions she raises in our minds, in response to this challenge, have to do with whether we are capable of teaching her fiction without institutionalizing it. That is, she asks us if we can teach *The Golden Notebook* without imposing a form and meaning on it that it does not have—whether we can teach her novel as a dialectic process and not as doctrine. In short, she asks if it is possible for us to teach her novel without, *ipso facto*, perverting her meaning and intentions in writing it. Finally, in challenging us so openly, it is as though she asks us if we dare teach this novel at all. In this paper I shall address these issues and argue that *The Golden Notebook* is a book eminently suited—if not designed—for teaching. Furthermore, I shall argue that when we teach this novel we function much as Lessing's own narrators do—that is, as mediators between her readers and the alternate realities of her fictional worlds.[1]

Before addressing the basic problem of this paper, however, I think it pertinent to raise the question of why Lessing is so mistrustful of teachers and critics. Some of the reasons she alludes to in the preface itself, where she makes reference to what she considers to have been misreadings of her novel. In this context, she is particularly sensitive to the fact that her "book was instantly belittled, by friendly reviewers as well as by hostile ones, as being about the sex war. . . ."[2] She explains her overreaction to this simplistic and, in her view, mistaken criticism by saying that she, like other authors, longs for what she calls "the perfect critic," the author's alter ego, "that other self more intelligent than oneself who has seen what one is reaching for, and who judges you only by whether you have matched up to your aim or not" (p. xv). In other words, she seeks in critics what Samuel R. Delany calls the "mythological audience of one"—that ideal reader for and to whom one writes.[3] Even beyond what Delany seems to have in mind as an ideal reader is Lessing's unspoken wish to be read by those who can help her with what she is doing. Another way of putting it would be to say that she seeks in critics and their critical response a continuation of the dialectical process that she has set up in her texts. That critics are unable "to provide what they purport to provide"—that is, a sympathetic, intelligent reading—Lessing ascribes to their education, which she claims trains them "in the opposite direction" (p. xv).

According to Lessing, the British (and one presumes American) educational system is one of indoctrination, by which individuals are made subordinate to authority. By teaching students to doubt their own judgment, the schools, in her view, are turning out critics and reviewers (and ultimately teachers) who are incapable of understanding her work. This failure on the part of the schools is particularly grating to Lessing, I would argue, because Lessing herself is—if one is bold enough to label her—preeminently a teacher. And, as I have implied, her method of teaching is not didactic but Socratic, by which she engages her readers in a progressive dialogue that leads them through a series of multiple realities to a new view of the world.

Although the teaching methods she employs are basically Socratic, the particular forms they take in her fiction come to her from two additional sources, the literature of Sufism and the philosophy of Marxism. From the Sufi canon she has learned the art of teaching indirectly, through parables and what the Sufis call teaching stories—conundrums that the reader must work through and meditate on in order to extract their meaning.[4] From Marxism she has learned the related art of dialectical thinking, whereby her readers through intellectual engagement with the text move from a series of contradictions and paradoxes to alternate levels of reality. As a proponent and practitioner of this Socratic method of instruction, Lessing would subvert our world view and our certainties by posing us difficult questions about the nature of reality. Her purpose in writing, therefore, is not to convince us of the validity of her ideas—the absolute existence of another world or level of reality—but to develop our ability to see beyond ourselves. And because she is convinced that critics and teachers, because of their own training, are unable to pursue this method of instruction, it is perfectly reasonable that she wants to address her readers without pedagogic interference on our part.

Given her mistrust of teachers and her outright condemnation of the educational system of which we are a part—a mistrust and condemnation she demonstrates in her fiction as well as in her preface—it seems to me that, if we are going to accept her challenge and teach *The Golden Notebook* (or any Lessing novel for that matter), we must use it as it was intended to be used: as a dialectical teaching story designed to subvert and thus transform our perceptions of the world. That is to say, we, as teachers, must accept the fact that when we teach Doris Lessing's fiction, we are engaging in a political activity. It is, of course, arguable that whenever we teach any literature, we are engaged in a political activity. Corroboration for this point of view can be found in Northrop Frye's monograph, *On Teaching Literature*, in which he remarks that "all scholarship is in a sense political; if it claims to be disinterested, it is really only defending the status quo."[5] It also can be found in the essays of the Marxist feminist critic, Lillian S. Robinson, in which she argues that neither literature nor criticism is value-free (see her collected essays, *Sex, Class, and Culture*).[6] As literary critics, both Frye and Robinson reflect the views of sociologists Peter L. Berger and Thomas Luckmann who argue in *The Social Construction of Reality: A Treatise in the Sociology of Knowledge* that language can function as "the objective repository of vast accumulations of meaning and experience, which it can then preserve in time and transmit to following generations."[7] In effect, according to Berger and Luckmann, language and, by extension, literature, are the most powerful socializing agents available to a particular culture.

That Lessing herself is cognizant of the socializing capabilities of language and literature is evident in even a cursory glance at her fiction. In *Martha Quest*, for example, Lessing informs us that Martha's view of the world has been determined largely by her reading. In *Briefing for a Descent into Hell*, Lessing demonstrates the discrepancies between the world view of her protagonist and that of the medical profession by constructing a language barrier between them. For example, her hero, Charles Watkins, who is on a metaphysical and schizophrenic journey to the interior, speaks in metaphors, paradoxes, and rich imagery; his thoroughly matter-of-fact and pedestrian physicians, who speak only literally, hear in what he says only lies and contradictions instead of unities. That the power of the language is vested only in those who have control of it, Lessing illustrates in *The Memoirs of a Survivor*, in which June Ryan, a young member of Britain's unemployed (and unemployable) lumpen proletariat, finds it impossible to communicate because she has virtually no language skills and only a very limited vocabulary. For June's handicap and impoverished language Lessing blames the educated class, who have "never found a way of sharing" the richness of language "with the lower reaches of our society."[8] That is, the ruling class is the educated class.

As Lessing is well aware, when language and literature are institutionalized, they become tools of the state. This institutionalization can take various forms. It can be as blatant as a state-controlled press or state-sponsored propaganda in an authoritarian (or totalitarian) society. Or it can be as subtle as the images and stories that dominate the cultural mythology of our own democratic society—and, in dominating it, give form to our collective fears and desires. Or, as recent feminist scholars have demonstrated, it can reside in the very language itself, where it acts to socialize individual men and women into stereotypical patterns of behavior. One of the most effective forms of socialization, as Lessing is well aware, is the school system itself. This, of course, brings us back to the question of why Lessing so distrusts teachers and provides us with perhaps our best explanation of why she prefers her work not be taught. Which is simply this: because she is writing literature that would subvert the system, she doesn't want it taught by those whose job, by definition, is to maintain it. In Lessing's view, teachers more often than not are in the rear guard of social change. Rather than liberating their students from ignorance, they are, to use her words, indoctrinating them into a repressive way of thinking.

If language and literature are used by society to socialize its members and control its deviants (as Lessing suggests they are, in her continued attacks on our propensity to label, pigeonhole, and dispose of people), they can also be used by those who, like Lessing herself, would transform society. These social reformers may have the same tools—language and literature—but they do not have the same reach as those in power. Thus their attempts at reform are often doomed from the start because the state, with very little effort, is able, in effect, to outshout these so-called troublemakers. In a closed society, like the Soviet Union, those dissidents who do speak out usually find themselves declared mentally incompetent and subsequently institutionalized for what is purportedly their own and society's well-being. Even in an open society, like our own and Great Britain's, dissidents risk imprisonment in jail or mental institutions. More commonly, because their message is unwelcome, these reformers, like the Old Testament prophets, risk public scorn and censure. In the case of a writer, this scorn can take the form of critical attack in the press. More subtly, perhaps, it can take the form of scholarly and pedagogic neglect, in which case the author's work is neither studied nor taught. One of the far-reaching consequences of this kind of neglect is that the author loses generation after generation of potential readers and sympathizers.

As I have already indicated, in choosing to use her fiction as an instrument of social criticism and change, Doris Lessing has drawn on the teaching models of Marxism and Sufism. In *The Golden Notebook* these influences are most notable in the dialectical structure of the novel. It is through this structure that Lessing avoids the pitfalls of most proletarian fiction of the 1930s, which was nothing more than thinly disguised propaganda for the Marxist revolution. As a teaching device, proletarian fiction failed in its intentions to revolutionize society because it preached without educating, by placing content above form—by ignoring its own dialectical method. Unlike the writers of proletarian fiction (whose work she mocks in the red notebooks), Lessing utilizes the Marxist model of dialectical progression by setting up a dialectical relationship between her text and her readers, whereby her readers learn how to escape institutionalized thought. She accomplishes this less by what she says to her readers than by what she does with them. That is, taking her cue from the Sufis, she has constructed in *The Golden Notebook* a novel whose very shape makes "a wordless statement" about the conventional novel and society itself (p. xiv).

What Lessing is saying through the dialectical structure of her novel is that the complexities and uncertainties of twentieth-century life can no longer be accommodated by the conventional novel. She makes her point by including in her text an example of a conventional novel, that is, the "Free Women" sections. Of all the sections, the five "Free Women" ones are by far the most orderly and simplistic versions of what happens to Anna Wulf, the protagonist. Because they do not reflect adequately the anguish and fragmentation that Anna experiences, they are ultimately unsatisfactory accounts of her life. But because they do not appear in isolation but in the context of other equally incomplete accounts, they do contribute to our understanding of this complex and tormented woman.

If they are inadequate as psychological truth, the "Free Women" sections do illustrate the dangers of submitting to a fatal nostalgia for meaning and order, a nostalgia that Lessing obviously fears—and obviously desires. It is a nostalgia that pervades all her fiction and one that Albert Camus describes in *The Myth of Sisyphus* as a "nostalgia for unity, that appetite for the absolute," which he finds characteristic of the "human drama" itself in its perennial longing for understanding and order.[9] This longing for form is so central to the human experience that according to Camus it is tempting to see in others' lives "a coherence and unity which they cannot have in reality, but which seem evident to the spectator."[10] This desire for unity seems to describe the dilemma that Anna has in perceiving her own life, whether she is looking back on it, as in the black notebooks' account of her African experiences, or trying to record it synchronically, as in the blue notebooks' account of her daily activities. The problems she has with recording her past she summarizes by observing that everything she remembers "was chosen by Anna, of twenty years ago" and she doesn't "know what this Anna of now would choose" (p. 137). In the dream that she has while she is writing the inner golden notebook, she summarizes the kinds of problems she has been having all along when she says, "I was unable to distinguish between what I had invented and what I had known, and I knew that what I had invented was all false" (pp. 619-20). The problems she has with recording her present life are exemplified in the experience she has when she tries to record objectively all the events of a single day in September 1954. During the writing she becomes aware of the fact that she is modifying the experience simply by scrutinizing it, when she says, "the idea that I will have to write it down is changing the balance, destroying the truth" (p. 341). After using several pages (from 331 to 368 in the paperback edition) to describe this day, Anna scores out the entire passage and replaces it with a single terse paragraph in which she condenses the day's events into nine sentences (p. 368). (On a less obvious plane, this is what she does throughout the novel when she alternates the four notebooks with the "Free Women" sections.)

The dilemma that Anna faces in trying to record her life is one faced by historians who charge themselves with the task of describing the past with accuracy and objectivity. Just as it is impossible for historians to view the world directly—without the distortion brought on by their methodology, purpose, and point of view—it is impossible for Anna to see herself clearly. Moreover, in recording her life, whether as fact or as fiction, she runs into the problem that in giving her life shape (order, form) and meaning, she is, by definition, falsifying it by transforming the meaningless fragments of her daily activities into a meaningful whole. She is perhaps most aware of this when she remarks at the end of the first installment of the yellow notebook that she has written the story of Paul and Ella "in terms of analysis of the laws of dissolution of the relationship between" them. She has done this because, as she says, "As soon as one has lived through something, it falls into a pattern" (p. 227). The problem is that her novel, *qua* literature, has form and meaning which her life—and the life of her characters—lacks. Although she has experienced the fragments she records, she has experienced them precisely as fragments and not as parts of a whole, meaningful existence. It is this absurdity that seems to be at the heart of *The Golden Notebook* and the source of Anna's writer's block.

Although Anna claims she writes in four notebooks for the very reason that she cannot write the kind of holistic novel she wants to (p. 61), what she does write is an honest account of the fragmentation she feels. Thus in each of her four notebooks and in the frame tale itself, Anna is presenting separate views of herself, discrete roles that she plays as she encounters the complex, opaque world of the twentieth century. In the separate sections, Anna demonstrates her own and the world's fragmentation; in the book itself, Anna (and ultimately Lessing) demonstrates the integration of these fragments that she has sought for so many years. (The integration is made possible by the breakdown in the inner golden notebook, but it is anticipated in the notebooks themselves, as Anna begins to confuse them in her own mind.) The paradox inherent in this novel is that its wholeness is composed of fragments. Because reading is basically a linear activity, we first experience the fragmentation or the details of Anna's life. Once we have finished reading and can look back on what we have read, we begin to see the unity they constitute. Thus we, at this point, reflect—or even in a sense repeat—what Anna herself has done in assembling the book.

As narrator of the entire text, Anna has been responsible for writing the individual sections and for putting them together to make a final statement about herself, the world, and the novel. What she has done is to give us a metaphor of herself, the world, and the novel. As other critics have ably pointed out, no one part of *The Golden Notebook* contains the "truth" or represents reality per se.[11] Instead, each of the major sections (the frame tale and the notebooks) provides a metaphor for all the others.[12] That is, in a metaphorical sense, "Free Women" is the black notebook is the red notebook is the yellow notebook is the blue notebook is the golden notebook. Moreover, as Max Black observes of the two terms of a metaphor, when we say A is B, we are saying something about A (it is B) and simultaneously something about B (it is A).[13] To use an example from the novel, if Anna is Ella, Ella is also Anna. In other words, Anna is no more real than Ella, and Ella is no more fictional than Anna (whether Anna appears in one of the notebooks or in "Free Women"). Ultimately, there is no distinction between fiction and reality in this novel.

Nor is there a single, uniform account of who Anna-Ella is and what she has done. Instead, we are supplied with a series of alternate routes through one woman's psyche. Although it might be tempting, for the sake of simplicity, to take each route (the frame tale and the notebooks) one at a time to its end, the book is not structured this way.[14] It is structured so that we are forced, willy-nilly, to switch tracks so often that we tend to become confused over what we have encountered where. Nor does it make it easy for us that Lessing has peppered her text with conflicting information, calculated to remind us that there is no final reality in the novel.

This destruction of our everyday reality seems to have been Lessing's purpose in writing *The Golden Notebook*. In destroying our old realities she is able to introduce us to new ones and thus to free us from our limited (and limiting) perceptions and preconceptions about the world. Unlike a conventional novel, which functions as a fairly accurate representation of the world as an orderly and, finally, comprehensible place, Lessing's novel functions to subvert this view of reality. Through the metaphor of her fiction, we learn that the meaning of the world eludes us if we try, by institutionalizing or labeling it, to pin it down. In other words, according to Lessing, we can only experience the world—we cannot explain it.

In teaching Lessing, therefore, we state—implicitly, if nothing else—that there are several ways of looking at the world, that no one social, religious, or political institution has a monopoly on truth. In teaching Lessing, we mediate between the closed world of contemporary society and the open world of her fiction. Like her narrators, we can help guide our students—her readers—on a dialectical journey through her amazing text, to the image of wholeness and unity that lies at the center of her fiction. In effect, in teaching Lessing, we are exchanging, if only briefly, our version of reality for her vision of reality. What we are given then, in teaching Lessing, is the opportunity to replace the teaching of dogma with the teaching of methodology. That is, rather than teaching our students what to think, we are teaching them how to think. Rather than indoctrinating them, we are educating them in the original sense of leading them out of themselves and the world they know. Teaching Doris Lessing, therefore, is a subversive activity, one that denies the power of institutions by asserting the rights of individuals to see the world on their own terms. It is also an activity that Lessing herself should welcome as part of her strategy to transform our perceptions and thus the world.

NOTES

1. For a discussion of Lessing's narrators as mediators, see my paper, "The Eye of the Storm: Narrative Technique in the Science Fiction of Doris Lessing," presented at the Modern Language Association convention, Houston, Texas, 30 Dec. 1980.

2. Doris Lessing, "Introduction" to *The Golden Notebook* (New York: Bantam, 1973), viii. All references are to this edition; subsequent page numbers appear in parentheses in the text. The Introduction is reprinted in *A Small Personal Voice* (New York: Alfred A. Knopf, 1974) in which it is identified as a "Preface." It is dated in the Bantam edition as June 1971.

3. Samuel R. Delany, *Nova* (New York: Bantam, 1969), 178.

4. On this subject, see Nancy Shields Hardin, "The Sufi Teaching Story and Doris Lessing," *Twentieth-Century Literature* 23, no. 3 (October 1977): 314-26.

5. Northrop Frye, *On Teaching Literature*, (New York: Harcourt Brace Jovanovich, 1972).

6. Lillian S. Robinson, *Sex, Class and Culture* (Bloomington: Indiana University Press, 1978).

7. Peter L. Berger and Thomas Luckmann, *The Social Construction of Reality: A Treatise in the Sociology of Knowledge* (Garden City, N.Y.: Anchor Books, 1967), 37.

8. Doris Lessing, *The Memoirs of a Survivor* (New York: Alfred A. Knopf, 1975), 110.

9. Albert Camus, *The Myth of Sisyphus and Other Essays*, trans. Justin O'Brien (New York: Vintage Books, 1955), 13.

10. Albert Camus, *The Rebel: An Essay on Man in Revolt*, trans. Anthony Bower (New York: Vintage Books, 1956), 13.

11. See, for example, Roberta Rubenstein's "Doris Lessing's *The Golden Notebook*: The Meaning of Its Shape," *American Imago* 31, no. 1 (Spring 1975): 40-58; and Mary Ann Singleton, *The City and the Veld: The Fiction of Doris Lessing* (Lewisburg, Pa.: Bucknell University Press, 1977), 83-99 passim.

12. On the subject of metaphor, see Valerie Carnes, " 'Chaos, that's the Point': Art as Metaphor in Doris Lessing's *The Golden Notebook*," *World Literature Written in English* 15, no. 1 (April 1976): 17-28.

13. Max Black, Chap. 3, "Metaphor," in his *Models and Metaphors: Studies in Language and Philosophy* (Ithaca, N.Y.: Cornell University Press, 1962), 25-47.

14. Betsy Draine successfully takes the novel apart in order to demonstrate its dynamics in "Nostalgia and Irony: The Postmodern Order of *The Golden Notebook*," *Modern Fiction Studies* 26, no. 1 (Spring 1980): 31-48.

Jeanne Murray Walker

Memory and Culture within the Individual: The Breakdown of Social Exchange in *Memoirs of a Survivor*

"We are living at a time which is so dangerous, violent, explosive, and precarious that it is in question whether soon there will be people left alive to write books and to read them," Doris Lessing has remarked. But the time in which people may still read can be lengthened, or at least its quality may be bettered, she believes, if writers create fictional portrayals of people acting responsibly in society. The individual and the collective—Lessing has stressed both sides of the equation. They are, she claims, precariously in balance in an age of dizzying change, always threatening to get out of kilter so that one overwhelms the other. It is the writer's task to portray "the responsible individual voluntarily submitting his will to the collective, but never finally; and insisting on making his own personal and private judgements before every act of submission."[1] There are two alternatives to this responsible blending of individuals into society. On the one hand, individuals may isolate themselves from one another, sulking or dreaming their separate dreams, egocentric but essentially helpless. On the other, people may allow themselves to be swept into large masses applauding or censoring without private imagination or individual choice, Lessing has claimed. It is therefore not surprising that one of the pivotal novels of her career as a novelist, *The Memoirs of a Survivor*, portrays both extremes—the ravaging, hysterical mob and the solipsistic, isolated individual—barely and slowly coming to terms with one another.

Lessing's own impassioned remarks suggest an interpretation of the work as a schematic portrayal of the negotiations among individuals.[2] Rather than showing these negotiations leading finally to a sane and productive collectivity, *Memoirs* refracts, like so many mirrors, the multiple kinds of exchange common in Western society in order to diagnose the breakdown of collectivity.[3] Against a backdrop of a city physically crumbling to ruin and the widespread "consciousness of something ending," Lessing sketches vignettes of failed exchange between individuals.[4] Each failure arises from its own particular causes. But clearly the immensity of human need is common to all. *Memoirs* shows that human beings cannot give back to others as much as they themselves use up merely to stay alive. Therefore, society's network of alliances, service, and commerce deteriorates. Social roles have become unstable, outmoded, and insufficient to allow satisfying contact between humans. And this creates the premonition that even more drastic change is impending.

Lessing emphasizes the problematic nature of the exchange between individuals in two ways. By tracing an individual psyche to the earliest exchanges that shaped it, she portrays the ongoing and fundamental problem that people are either stifled or left unrequited by human bonding. Parents fail to satisfy genuine needs of their young while imposing irrelevant demands. They must do so because although their own needs were left unmet, they were forced to give at someone else's demand, and so on, back through the generations in an infinite regress. Through the history of one individual, Lessing articulates and explains the inevitable, constant tenuousness of human exchange, the tendency of the bonding forces in society to weaken, to wear out, to break down altogether. But she also shows that at specific moments in certain countries human exchange is in such great danger of failing that the people in these societies are plagued by a sense of impending apocalypse.

And yet in *Memoirs* Lessing cannot give up on the collective, even though it exists not in the streets but only as an ideal in the realm of the mind. The scheme of the book portrays this realm as a place behind the narrator's living room wall to which she can sometimes retreat. As culture slides backward, reversing the stages of civilization, the narrator discovers that "two worlds," the public, social space, and the private, interior spaces of the mind, "lay side by side and closely connected. But then one life [excluded] the other and I did not expect the two worlds ever to link up" (p.25). At the end of the novel, a straggling huddle of cannibalistic children pins three adults in the narrator's apartment until finally the wall deteriorates altogether and everyone—even the children—escapes into the space behind the wall. This "link up" between the two worlds is Lessing's solution to the problem of exchange between people. In the healing of a fragmented human personality, in the narrator's finally seeing the connection between social acts, memory, and cultural thought, lies her own salvation and that of the group.

Lessing connects personal integration with social exchange by using one as a metaphor for the other. She characterizes personal integration as the drama of exchange between two separate individuals.[5] Emily, the developing, impulsive social activist side of a personality, is scrutinized with irony or tenderness or irritation by the narrator, the side which would, if left to its own devices, while away the hours reading or remembering the past. These two, Emily and the narrator, thrown into the same house without rhyme or reason, eye one another warily; slowly grope toward a language to use with one another; form ties; and, in spite of the narrator's constant fear that Emily will take off without her, eventually recognize that they *cannot* abandon one another: survival requires their mutual dependence. Although this is an allegory of psychological integration, it is also quite literally a story of two very different, separate human beings painstakingly forming a social bond. Faithfulness to Lessing's fiction requires that we take account of both the vehicle and the tenor, of both the social and psychological sides of the metaphorical equation.[6]

To preserve the complex relationship between the individual psyche and social collectivity in *Memoirs*, it is helpful to think of the events in the novel as ranging along two axes. One axis might be thought of as the relations among various aspects of one human psyche, the other as the social relations between one human being and another. Lessing manages to combine both these intrapersonal and interpersonal aspects in the relations between the two major characters, Emily and the narrator. On the one hand Emily must be read as the narrator, as *more* than a teenager with whom the narrator lives. Otherwise how could the narrator, who is certainly not omniscient, view scenes of Emily's past, which often take place in a bedroom filled with furniture the vintage of the narrator's own youth? On the other hand, Emily is most emphatically a character in her own right, an autonomous, impulsive teenager. This ambiguity at the very center of *Memoirs* allows Lessing to tether all she says in the novel to the assumption that connections within the human personality are like relationships between people.

Lessing explores the problematic nature of society in her depiction of exchange among individuals, and this series of episodes may be thought of as one axis of the novel. The work does not only portray the exchanges between the narrator and Emily, who is abruptly and mysteriously deposited in her living room. The novel also explores exchange between a child and its parent, between lovers, between female friends, among members of a socialist collective, among members of a welfare family, and even among members of a pack of savage children. The most important of these, and the only successful one, is the relationship between Emily and the narrator. But Lessing manages to sketch an example of all the major kinds of exchange, a fact that helps to dictate the schematic structure of the book and also contributes to its comprehensiveness as a social statement.[7]

The alarm and social malaise Lessing dramatizes in *Memoirs* is circular. Some time after "The Age of Affluence" good solid common citizens begin to detect the breakdown of society. Helpless to prevent its collapse, and filled with dread, the people either fail to carry out their own responsibilities or become ill. As a result, everything grows worse. Because it is so difficult to pinpoint when the deterioration started, deterioration seems both the inevitable and permanent condition of society. The universality of the novel's setting, "a city," adds to the sense that Lessing is making a general statement. Yet the particularity of the time—the future, sometime after the Age of Affluence—implies the dramatic worsening of social conditions in the modern age.

The cause of this worsening is referred to by the narrator as "It." Ignorance, the narrator calls it at one point (p. 153), but that definition doesn't keep its shape. "It," one ultimately realizes, is the exhausting demand that individuals place on the social structure, their need, and their inability to be satisfied. In each person's life this need produces different symptoms: "an illness, a tiredness, boils." In the collective it manifests itself as "the price and unreliability of the electric supply; the way telephones didn't work" (p. 158). More than anything else, the unsatisfied need is the need for social exchange.

This outrageous, thirsty need is filled for the middle class by the most vaporous and unsatisfying of all possible commodities: news. *Memoirs'* portrayal of "public services stopped, crops left in the fields, animals loose, food scarce, and gangs of adolescents roaming the streets" (p. 10) implies how great the real needs of society are. Yet news is the most important "currency" (p. 49) among people of the middle class who have neither joined the Authority nor yet chosen to migrate with one of the gangs. News, which really amounts to rumor swapping, is what gives these people their "identity." "Not getting it, or enough of it, deprived [them], made [them] anxious" (p. 50).

Not only is the most important commodity in the society unsatisfying; the Authority, which produces that useless commodity, demands much of the society's real, nourishing products in return for news. This unequal exchange explains why the Authority "is the most powerful of all mechanisms for society's undermining, its rotting, its collapse." The main rumor this class of people perpetuates is that "security, permanence, order" exist (p. 106), a rumor only too gladly "bought" by the middle class. Yet Lessing shows that the Authority possesses less, not more, ability than the gang's to survive as a social unit.

By failing to produce anything while they consume great quantities of goods, the Authority eventually isolate themselves. Society requires exchange, giving as well as receiving. The Authority have nothing but talk to give, and the middle class gradually begins to perceive the insubstantiality of talk, its failure to nourish them. Therefore, the people finally ignore them, hoping only to be left alone, and the Authority eventually have to leave the city like everyone else.

The alternative to exchanging news, a commodity with less and less substance, is the evenhanded exchange of real goods which takes place within the gangs. Although these gangs of roving young people are at first eyed with suspicion by the middle class, which is trying to perpetuate the "old forms" (p. 18), the narrator, under Emily's tutelage, slowly realizes their legitimacy as social organizations. As she remarks, they have a structure—"evolved under the pressures of necessity" (p. 106) to be sure, but it is a *structure*. "A short time with people living this sort of life and one grasped all the rules—all unwritten of course, but one knew what to expect" (p. 174). They themselves settle into status positions and live according to understandable laws. As Gerald's favorite, Emily becomes the chief woman. She lends her belief and competence to Gerald, who in turn spends his energy directing the group and finding supplies. Emily is repaid for her output by the adoration and obedience of the group's younger members. This kind of exchange does not differ markedly from the exchange in any group. What makes the gang seem different is that its form is not prescribed by Authority, and its members are deeply idealistic.

Yet even the gangs, which comprehend the need for new social forms, cannot long maintain real democracy or equality of status between men and women. The narrator recognizes that social patterning may be innate in human consciousness. When Gerald loiters on the pavement while Emily works in the gang's house, it seems to the narrator "the equivalent of a male going out to hunt" (p. 135). It distresses the narrator that "old patterns keep repeating themselves, re-forming themselves even when events seemed to license any experiment or deviation or mutation" (p. 136). It distresses her because she already has seen these very patterns lead to decadence and breakdown in middle-class adult society. If it is true that social patterns are fixed and inevitable, then progressive societies always mutate back to the same old forms, Lessing shows. This is the wisdom of a woman old enough to recognize repeated patterns when she sees them.

On the other hand, what distresses Emily, the young social activist, is that society consists of roles. Exchanges occur among people who fill roles and the roles can be filled by any of a number of people. To think about society in this way seems to leave no room for individual feeling or idiosyncratic personality. When Emily realizes that if she did not fill the role of dominant female "someone would" (p. 141), the narrator reacts with alarm, for this line of reasoning leads to suicide. These limitations—the inevitability of social patterns and the disinterested quality of social roles—become more and more apparent, even during the bloom and success of the collective.

And yet, despite this awareness, the desire to escape social patterns, if only for a time, continues to be a tantalizing fantasy. The narrator herself longs to join a gang and migrate even though she realizes that it would only mean a brief reprieve from social patterns. She fancies that before those patterns hardened,

> an earlier life of mankind would rule: disciplined, but democratic (when these people were at their best, even a child's voice was listened to with respect); all property worries gone; all sexual taboos gone (except for the new ones, but new ones are always more bearable than the old); all problems shared and carried in common. Free. Free, at least from what was left of "civilization" and its burdens. (p. 167)

It is the longing expressed in this view that pulls people into the streets and causes them to migrate to unknown regions. But the defects of this fantasy are revealed immediately in *Memoirs*.

Lessing's portrayal of the cannibalistic gang of children depicts what happens when social patterns do not rule exchanges among members of a social group. Unlike the adolescents in Gerald's and Emily's group, these children do not produce anything; they steal water and they kill—people, if necessary—for food. With them it is impossible to make a pact of friendship. If they know and have commerce with a person, that constitutes more, not less, reason to victimize him. They do not even have any loyalty toward one another. "They would be hunting in a group one hour, and murdering one of their number the next" (p. 75). They cannot be made to keep their own home clean, and if it were not for Emily, they would have killed Gerald, their leader and provider. In this portrayal of society without structure, Lessing deals harshly with the notion that humans can exist together free of social patterns. And yet all the collectives Lessing portrays in *Memoirs* leave Emily restless, unsatisfied, full of grief, and longing for something better.

Memoirs explicates the defects of social exchange by focusing on individual relationships. Two of the most promising of these are the relationships between lovers and that between female friends of the same age. Emily forms a bond with June which is closer than any other she experiences. The bond between these two bears the extreme test of their conflicting sexual interest in Gerald. Although Emily writhes with jealousy when Gerald chooses June over her for a period of time, that jealousy does not turn Emily against June. On the contrary, Emily feels acute longing for June's presence while June is with Gerald. She wails "But I miss her *now*" (p. 144).

Yet the bond between June and Emily doesn't prove permanent. Like many other women these days, Lessing implies, June cannot be made to understand that her gifts—her affection, her advice, her comfort, her work—are worthwhile. As her right to receive gifts follows from her ability to give them, she cannot be made to feel obligated. She suffers from a social dysfunction which is the opposite of Emily's. Instead of dutifully returning to the social system time after time, instead of trying repeatedly to establish contact, June merely drifts off. Lessing suggests that a major reason why social bonds between women fail is that, lacking the belief that they have given, they cannot be made to receive.

Emily's relationship with Gerald follows the arc that romantic, sexual relationships in our culture frequently take:

from euphoric amazement at the fact of having been chosen, through passionate, jealous self-doubts, to affectionate, dutiful, weary commitment. Lessing portrays the exchange from Emily's point of view; that is, at last, resigned disappointment. At first she believes the failure to be caused by her inappropriate desire to fill the old-fashioned, romantic role of female lover. Then she realizes that no role she or Gerald could fill for one another would satisfy her, no matter how well-meaning they both are. Her need simply exceeds his comprehension. "You don't value me," she complains. "You take me for granted" (p. 173). Genuinely loving and concerned to have Emily, Gerald remains bewildered by her accusations.

In the end, Emily gives more and gets less than either June or Gerald, and this is the reason, finally, why both relationships break down. Lessing's description of Emily's attitude toward Gerald makes this clear. "She has known it all, and doesn't want any more—but what can she do? She knows herself—the eyes of men and boys say so—as a source; if she is not this, then she is nothing. So she still thinks—she has not yet shed that delusion. She gives. She gives. But with this weariness held in check and concealed..." (p. 200).

It is tempting to say Lessing is concluding here that women have life hard and that is that. But to say so would be to miss the point. Emily's rage and bereavement are caused by her monstrous need. She is rapacious in her demands for affection, for loyalty, for attention, for obedience. It is only fair to say that she gives relentlessly in an effort to pay back, but she is simply unable to produce as much as she consumes. The narrator, her mother, Gerald, the children at the cooperative house, all find her impossible to satisfy. It is this that makes the narrator finally say of her, "What on earth, the observer has to ask—husband, lover, mother, friend...can you have possibly expected of me, of life that you can now cry like this" (p. 172). But Emily's failure is not uniquely hers. It is the widespread and general condition of society. The inability to produce as much as she consumes is finally the misery which the narrator calls "it," which terrifies all the people in *Memoirs* and causes the breakdown of the social system.

The only solution to Emily's failures of bonding, most lucid in Lessing's closeups of Emily's interpersonal relationships, is for the child to learn about her own past. This frees her to think about new ways of ordering her experience. In the last scene of the novel the narrator leads Emily, Gerald, and the children through the wall. Emily, who has been forced to attempt social exchange without either self-knowledge or the solace and ordering of a cultural vision, is finally able to see these realms. She cannot find them until she has run the gamut of social experiment, until the possibility of society itself has collapsed for her. Then the white wall breaks down, the wall which to Emily has represented frigidity and sterility in her nursery, but which has seemed to the narrator like an eggshell (see pp. 146-47) alive with potential. Behind the wall the group meet a woman, the presence that inhabits the realm, around whom people can cluster in free exchange. This presence shows them "the way out of this collapsed little world into another order or world altogether" (p. 217). The precise nature of this "other order" is not clear, but one thing is clear. It lies not in social experience but in the human imagination, in the capability of the individual to discover new ways of ordering human experience. For, as the narrator tells Emily, although everybody has to find a place in a social structure, such structure is "a trap and we're all in it" (p. 132).

The trap Emily falls into—needing more from society than she can get from it or give to it—that trap is sprung when Emily and the narrator become mutually dependent and self-sufficient at the end of the novel. All through *Memoirs* Lessing portrays the growing interdependence of the two—an image of the fragmented human psyche becoming whole and complete.[8] Emily brings things from the outside in to the narrator: her tribe, June, Gerald. In turn, the narrator reveals to Emily a realm that is interior, the space behind the wall. The process of this integration, how the peculiarities of the narrator and

Emily—which remain peculiarities—come to be the common property of both, is the heartbeat, the central axis of the story.

The child, Emily, functions in the novel as a personification of the narrator's own socialization process which the narrator observes and remembers as if it had been the external action of another person. Emily's unceremonious arrival and the intense but inexplicable feeling of responsibility she creates in the narrator (p. 24) prevent the narrator from spending all of her time in the space behind the wall. With helpless affection the narrator watches Emily comment cynically on people who pass the window, devour food, fret over her figure, moon over fashions in magazines, practice roles in front of the mirror, plunge into love with a young hero, storm and rail over his unfaithfulness, nurture others with a driven competence, and lose her best friend. All this the narrator observes as though by memory, attended by the unmistakable powerlessness and therefore nostalgia of the old reliving the acts that formed them. As the narrator comments, "we—everyone—will look back over a period of life, over a sequence of events, and find much more there than they did at the time" (p. 3).

By portraying Emily as the child who coaxes the narrator into an exchange first with her, then with others, Lessing describes not only Emily's but also the narrator's socialization. At first when Emily finds herself in the old woman's apartment she possesses only a sociable surface, the quick polished brightness she has adopted to hide emotion and to please her elders. In reality she is forlorn, isolated, eager to "be far away from the world" (p. 17), and her skill at social chit-chat makes it more difficult for her to carry on any exchange that is not formulaic. But eventually this constant, "awful need to be so bright and good" (p. 26) gives way, and she begins to use the narrator "to check her impulse to step forward away from childhood" (p. 48). The narrator is relieved to be so used. She relates to Emily's fantasies of farm life. Then to the narrator's delight, Emily sneaks one of the older woman's cherished blouses for a costume she has rigged up. By mimicking and criticizing everyone around her, Emily forces the narrator to realize her own condition, her isolation, her imprisonment. But eventually the social experiments begin. Emily slowly, reticently introduces the narrator to collective life, first in the street and then in Gerald's house. Without Emily the narrator would never have experienced this substantive reciprocity between people, in spite of her strong, almost desperate need for collective life. Eventually all the social experiments fail and civilization collapses around her. But even then the narrator realizes that Emily's counsel about how to survive is the more competent of the two. Because Emily is more practiced in the social world than the narrator, the narrator relinquishes to Emily the power to make choices about social arrangements for both of them. Lessing compresses the complete social development of a woman, from early adolescence to maturity, into her portrayal of Emily.

The narrator, on the other hand, represents the ability of the human personality to speculate, to contemplate, to fantasize. She is the one who supplies Emily material and makes sense of her violent moods. Although Emily eventually comes to feel affection for the narrator, she uses the narrator as the young use the old, with instinctive right and without much thought. Because the narrator is capable of distancing herself from the present, moving backward in time, through memory, she has access to older cultural forms. The fiction portrays this by presenting her as the owner of a treasure house of objects—furs, fabric, a sewing machine, a toaster—and social forms—memories of romantic love, for example, and idyllic stories of life on the farm.

These cultural objects and social forms Emily usurps to make use of any way she can. She enjoys the fantasies for the bygones they are. She refashions the clothes to fit her needs and trades in the electric objects for useful pots and pans. Meanwhile the narrator, whose story is really in a major sense the comings and goings of Emily, explains the child's emotions with a shrewdness and insight of which Emily, who is all action, is not capable. This is the narrator's role: to make sense of the action, the exchanges between people. And yet it is a role so apparently passive that the narrator comments at one point, "I almost felt myself not to exist, in my own right" (p. 27). She admits that she spends most of her life "simply waiting" (p. 102).

What keeps Emily from subsuming the entire story, swallowing the narrator up in furious activity, is the narrator's repeated journeys to the place behind the wall. Behind the living room wall two realms exist; the narrator apparently has no control over when she goes behind the wall or over which of the realms she visits. One she calls "the personal." That realm is furnished with Edwardian furniture and populated usually, but not always, by Emily and her immediate family. The other realm is a garden and a faintly familiar set of rooms, all in need of repair, which alternate unpredictably. Emily acts, blithely unaware of either the personal or the cultural realm.

One of these rooms might be thought of as cultural activity, as a place where the mind can shape experience according to some system other than memory or an order supplied by the past. This realm is a turmoil of smells and sights, flowers and herbs in the garden, styles and conditions of furniture in the rooms. Although it frequently needs drastic tidying, the narrator feels there "a lightness, a freedom, a feeling of possibility." Not only does she sense the presence of a loving inhabitant who will approve of her scrubbing and painting, but she also feels released by "the space and the possibility of alternative action" (p. 42). In this realm, Lessing has portrayed a spatialized image of art and religion, of cultural activity, activity in which the ego is orderer rather than ordered. Furthermore, although the forms of the objects in this realm are products of history, they are not irreversibly defined. The narrator is free to reshape them and by doing so to revise the effects of time. In contrast, the other realm is a place where time is irreversible, where its effects are necessary and inescapable. There the human ego is shaped by its surroundings instead of shaping them. Walls, other people, food, clothes—everything—impinges on the human ego, demanding or forbidding response, dominating and ordering. The clock, particularly, is "obeyed by everyone, consulted, constantly watched" (p. 43). Therefore, it becomes the sinister symbol of this second realm, "the personal," where Emily was structured irrevocably by her earliest response.

However unaware Emily may be of the "personal," of her own past, it does of necessity influence her. The sense of isolation she must work so hard to avoid began in childhood where objects were too big, her nurse's hands too rough, and where she constantly saw all her parents' love going to her baby brother. Her control and repression arose from the awesome, frigid whiteness of her nursery and the deprivation such whiteness suggests, as well as from her rigid schedule of feedings. Her need to take care of the young and the weak grew out of her belief that her parents had actually given her baby brother to her. Her inability to be satisfied by nourishing others, the sense that she is put upon and unappreciated for all her effort, derived from her mother, who endlessly complained of her lot. Both Emily's capability as an "authority" and her dismay at that capability also derived from long years of watching her mother, who was always in chilly control. Conversely, Emily's unwillingness to turn herself over completely to Gerald or to any man is the result of her father's sadistic and unmistakably sexual tickling bouts with her. Emily has been patterned by her past. That is unquestionable. But because she cannot see her past, she cannot understand its limiting effect upon her social exchanges. This lack of knowledge itself constitutes part of her entrapment.

It is the narrator who understands that Emily's attitudes and behavior are the result of what goes on in the "personal." On one occasion the narrator is obsessed, driven mad by the continual, miserable sobbing which she believes is Emily's, coming from behind the wall. She turns to Emily and asks, "Can't you hear someone crying?" Emily answers, "No, can you?" and walks away (p. 149). Because Emily cannot see her past as the cause of her present behavior, she cannot modify her choices. In order to thoughtfully choose among alternative responses to the people and things around her, rather than automatically falling into patterns dictated by her past, she must possess a consciousness of that past, as the narrator does. In fact, when Lessing portrays the narrator as a spectator in the realm of "the personal," she portrays Emily at a later stage, remembering her own childhood patterning, at last comprehending the cause of her social experiments and their failures.

The realm of "the personal" traces not only Emily's social patterning but that of her ancestors as well. The narrator hears the wailing of Emily's mother and other unidentified babies who have been denied love, going back through generations. These weeping, unconsoled, and inconsolable babies are "the world's image" according to the narrator; they are the mothers who will in turn deny love to their children, creating such indelible need within them that it makes social exchange difficult and jeopardizes the possibility of society itself. No wonder the narrator feels that "to enter the 'personal' [is] to enter a prison." It is the finished, determined past, where "time [is] a strict, unalterable law" (p. 42), and the need created there cannot be undone.

On the one hand, Lessing's story of Emily and the narrator portrays the inevitably problematic nature of human exchange: the past has impinged on each of us in a way which leaves us incapable of giving enough to others so that they, in turn, can satisfy our needs. On the other hand, it is possible precisely by understanding the past to become capable of ordering, of *re*-ordering. One can never re-order the *events* of one's own past, but it is possible to order one's own nature by reordering the forms which surround it. These are represented by the garden and the period furniture in the first realm behind the wall.

It is the interdependence between Emily and the narrator that finally grants this limited ordering power. By herself, the narrator remains isolated and contemplative; by herself, Emily returns again and again to social experiences that never satisfy her. Combining the characteristics of Emily and the narrator at the end of the book, where the two face a mob of savage children, Lessing portrays the need to mediate between the extremes of solipsistic individualism and rash, mindless collectivity. Together, Emily and the narrator become introspective, shrewd about their own survival, and capable of sheltering others.

Such integration requires that time be thought of as organic unfolding, Lessing shows, for the triumph is finally achieved by the elderly narrator. It is in her realm that the fragments are brought together. For Emily, time is external and arbitrary, merely measured by the clock which is either irrelevant or contrary to her own desires. But time for the narrator occurs as her own experience, as the stages which will bring to fruition something for which she waits. She is able to stop futilely exerting her own ego because she comprehends time as the maturation of natural things; therefore, nothing could be accomplished by a deliberate attempt of the "will" (p. 151). This attitude is typical of those who have lived a long time, and Lessing suggests that the vantage point of age is necessary for human integration.

Lessing's metaphor of Emily and the narrator—distinct individuals of two different ages and temperaments—allows her to dramatize *both* the integration of a human psyche and an idealized model of social exchange. One discovers by reading *Memoirs* how understanding one's own former or future self is like understanding another. The narrator understands the meaning of Emily's action because she can remember her own adolescence and social experiments. Indeed, in one sense, Emily *is* the narrator's remembered adolescence.

In contrast, the youthful Emily has no real insight into the narrator's behavior. As the narrator comments—about Emily but also about her own adolescent view of herself as an old woman—she sees no more "than an elderly person, with the characteristics to be expected of one" (p. 47). Yet one-dimensional as adolescence and early adulthood may be, they are a valid stage, "every bit as valid as the one ahead" (p. 94). If the narrator had been denied reciprocity with Emily, she would never have become fully integrated; her going through the wall would have been mere escape. Thus, Lessing depicts the need for exchange between individuals with the very metaphor which shows that ultimate salvation comes only to individuals who can achieve wholeness within themselves.

However neatly Lessing may package the social with the psychological in this novel, the ending appears puzzling. Some readers may feel shortchanged because the conclusion seems escapist. Characters who have had to scramble for food and compete for shelter in an increasingly threatening society are allowed at the end of the novel to take refuge behind a wall. And Lessing's insistence that this realm is more "real" than everyday reality doesn't do much to quiet the reader who feels disappointed by the conclusion (p. 162).

But the ending does follow faithfully from images and ideas which precede it. In the first place, although it arrives abruptly, it comes no more suddenly than most of the other scenes in the novel. More importantly, it grows out of both the aesthetics and the intellectual structure of the novel. The intellectual problem which the novel sets up in sharp relief is the possibility that the system of exchange among individuals may break down because the needs of people exceed their ability to receive or pay back to other people. The need for food is the major image in which Lessing expresses this threat to the social system. She solves this problem consistently, in the aesthetic terms which set it up.

The food metaphor which runs through *Memoirs* articulates the novel's central problem, the problem of excessive individual need.[9] In a stage like hibernation which precedes her social experiments, Emily drives the narrator wild by lying on the floor, her jaws constantly moving, eating, eating. When she stops literally devouring food she begins consuming the culture. She takes in "other people, atmospheres, events, places as though she were swallowing [them] whole" (p. 55). These things rapidly go through her as she is left empty and desperate for more material. Emily's desperation to participate in social exchange is sharply contrasted with June's inability to eat. June frustrates Emily, and Emily tries to force-feed her. But that only leads to June's disappearance. June's response is a typical response to Authority, for as the narrator shrewdly observes, Emily is an Authority. Her increasing demands cause others to leave.

In the end, Emily's need tyrannizes not only others, but herself as well. One aspect of Emily's need is that she must be continually active, without reprieve, in order to get enough from others to sustain herself. Even then she cannot be satisfied, as the narrator's dream of eating a sugar house with Emily emphasizes: "one could eat and never be filled" (p. 145). Existence equals consumption and nothing else in this scene. Another aspect of the tyranny Emily feels is her inability to produce anything sufficiently worthwhile to cover her costly consumption, to pay back society for what she takes from it. This inability is most clearly expressed in alimentary images. Emily's guilt over her inability is exacerbated in the scene of the "personal" where her mother scolds "You are a naughty girl, Emily, naughty, naughty, naughty, disgusting, filthy, dirty..." (p. 146). Far from repaying her mother or anyone else for her consumption, she irritates them by her products. That is the realization to which she is "condemned" (p. 68).

But food is not Lessing's most important image of actual objects consumed or exchanged; in fact skillful making of and bartering for objects within Emily's and Gerald's collective introduces the solution to Emily's inexhaustible need and her inability to return enough to society. The collective considers the problem of consumption seriously and intelligently. Its leaders plant a garden and set children to practice the old arts of weaving, sewing, and cooking. The children are vigorous and inventive and resourceful "in ways of [the] hand-to-mouth world" (p. 166). They figure the worth of a commodity according to its ability to fill a need and "things [do] not belong to people as they once did" (p. 119).

What is important about this attitude toward objects is that it is cultural; it emphasizes commonality and it thinks about objects at the level of the past. Not only do the children return to the old arts; they also take apart now useless toasters and other electrical equipment so that they can integrate the parts into new objects of real use. The world is filled with plenty of material for them to take apart; junkyards abound. The children see this and realize that the important task of human beings lies not in generating material but in re-forming it. And this is the sort of activity behind the wall to which Lessing points as the solution to Emily's great need.

Behind the wall, gardens are alive with fertility; there is a copious plenty which must only be harvested. Using the metaphor of food, Lessing solves the problem in the same terms in which she originally set it. "The food-giving surfaces of the earth doubled, trebled, endless—the plenty of it, the richness, the generosity . . ." (p. 161). The place behind the wall offers such promise of bounty that even Emily with her voracious need cannot possibly consume it all. Although gleaning such plenty requires tremendous energy, it repays that output lavishly. That is why the narrator "feels that most vivid expectancy when she goes there" (p. 12).

The garden metaphor solves the problem of excessive hunger which plagues Emily but not in the terms in which Emily had defined it. The garden does not signify unlimited social transactions; it does not signify satisfaction derived from social exchange at all. On the contrary, it suggests the plentitude of nature—of one's own ripening nature, of patience with one's own slow, developing completeness. The bounty of nature extends to the human psyche, Lessing argues. In time, the fractured elements of a human personality can gather and combine into a mature, reflexive whole.

The metaphor of furniture in the rooms, all of it antiquated or stained or slashed, on the other hand, presents an image of the possibilities that lie in re-ordering cultural forms and traditions. Here too is an inexhaustible supply of material; Emily doesn't have to fear using it up as one must fear using too much in social exchange. The forms of culture—houses, rooms, paint, patterns of furniture and rugs—exist in abundance. Furthermore, in this realm violence and destruction are not terrifying. They are exhilarating. If it were not for the fact that cultural forms become exhausted, used up, worn out with time and rejected, there would be no chance to reformulate them. So the narrator revels in the spirit of anarchy that blows through the realm behind the wall. It is that spirit that leaves the rooms a chaos of possibility, that allows her ego to exert itself freely at last (p. 110).

The narrator's experiments in the rooms behind the wall supplement social exchange with a more satisfying order of exchange. Whereas social forms seem unvarying and permanent and therefore incapable of being produced or changed, cultural forms are endlessly variable. Whereas the products of society —food, fabric, electrical gadgets—are quickly consumed and must be replaced, art and religion are not consumable. Behind the wall the inexhaustible supply of material and the real possibility of shaping that material make the individual capable of being productive. But Lessing also shows that individuals need to be productive to be whole. Although social exchange often leaves people feeling hopelessly in debt and unproductive, cultural activity allows them to feel productive and thus deserving the gifts of others. The realm behind the wall, therefore, leads to a personal fulfillment not possible through social exchange alone.

The retreat behind the wall is not an escape from social exchange, which of course cannot be escaped; in fact Lessing demonstrates the power of the cultural realm to order social experience. This is portrayed in a scene where the narrator wanders into a hexagonal room. There, strangers lay down bits of fabric at random which together create a rug with a handsome design. This is the "central activity" in the place behind the wall, uniting different people with different goals in "loving cooperation" (p. 80). Such community is an ideal, of course, which does not exist in the "personal." It is a vision of community loose and devoid of social roles but united through the human need and power to order, to find a pattern, a meaning which transcends time.[10] The fact that Lessing finally pushes her characters out of the book's present time into this realm suggests her belief in the power and the immanence of this vision. Yet it is still a vision, a model, if you will, of community, created by the ordering power of the narrator.

What is at stake in *Memoirs* is survival. What is necessary for survival? Both the individual and the collective, Lessing shows. First she shows that survival depends on reciprocity, integration, commerce between the different aspects of one personality. A person must understand her own historical development as cause and effect. But she must be able to escape the necessities that understanding creates by imaginative reciprocity with other cultural periods and with schemes of order other than the historical. In addition to these requirements for personal survival, Lessing shows that reciprocity among individuals is essential if society is to survive. And she maintains that society as well as the individual *can* survive, although in a curtailed form. However, because of the inordinate demands that social reciprocity makes on individuals and the minimal way it supplies needs, it is necessary for society as well as for the individual constantly to reformulate social ideals. This reformulation takes place in the realm behind the wall, the realm of art and religion. That is the place, after all, from which *The Memoirs of a Survivor* is written.

NOTES

1. Doris Lessing, "The Small Personal Voice," in *A Small Personal Voice*, ed. Paul Schlueter (New York: Alfred A. Knopf, 1974), 7, 12.

2. An effort has been made to interpret *Memoirs of a Survivor* in Jungian terms, and although this study is helpful, it downplays Lessing's clear concern about the state of society. See Roberta Rubenstein, *The Novelistic Vision of Doris Lessing: Breaking the Forms of Consciousness* (Urbana: University of Illinois Press, 1979), 220-42. See also Lorelie Cederstrom, " 'Inner Space' Landscape: Lessing's *Memoirs*," *Mosaic* 13, Spring/Summer (1980): 117, who argues that the landscape of *Memoirs* is an internal landscape and "the realistic level of the novel . . . is a symbolic portrait of the ego in a time of cultural failure." Cederstrom also relies heavily on Jung for her interpretation.

3. Guido Kums, "Apocalypse and Utopia in Doris Lessing's *The Memoirs of a Survivor*," *The International Fiction Review* 7, no. 2 (1980): 79-84, traces this theme of cultural crisis through several Lessing novels.

4. Doris Lessing, *The Memoirs of a Survivor* (New York: Bantam, 1975), 154. All references are to this edition; subsequent page references appear in parentheses in the text.

5. Mary Ann Singleton, *The City and the Veld: The Fiction of Doris Lessing* (Lewisburg, Pa.: Bucknell University Press, 1977), 19, shows that Lessing habitually portrays "strife-torn society" in contrast with a "new and more unified form of consciousness" brought about by "the human imagination."

6. Betsy Draine has argued that Lessing uses Marxist, Jungian, and Sufi theories to frame in concrete, mental, and spiritual realities in the novel and that these frames are finally unconvincing because they are too schematic. See her "Changing Frames: Doris Lessing's *Memoirs of a Survivor*," *Studies in the Novel* 11, no. 1 (Spring 1979): 51-62. I wish to argue here that Lessing's fiction in *Memoirs of a Survivor* is allegorical in the way Spenser's *Faerie Queene* is allegorical; that a single image in the novel often signals both social and psychological meaning.

7. Bernard Duyfhuizen extends the novel's concern with exchange by arguing that the novel is primarily a comment on novelistic conventions. See his "On the Writing of Future-History: Beginning the Ending in Doris Lessing's *Memoirs of a Survivor*," *Modern Fiction Studies* 26, no. 1 (Spring 1980): 147-56. See also Alvin Sullivan, "*The Memoirs of a Survivor*: Lessing's Notes toward a Supreme Fiction," in the same issue, pp. 157-62.

8. Rubenstein, *Novelistic Vision*, p. 238.

9. Lessing's use of food and the gardens which produce food as a dominant metaphor in *Memoirs of a Survivor* is not surprising, for nature, or fertility, is a metaphor which reverberates throughout her work. See Singleton, *City and the Veld*, 50-76.

10. The philosophy of unity expressed in this image is that of Sufism, which is visionary and mystical. But *whatever* its specific philosophical derivation, my point is that it is a product of cultural activity, of religious and artistic thought. See Rubenstein, *Novelistic Vision*, 120-23.

ELIZABETH ABEL

Resisting the Exchange: Brother-Sister Incest in Fiction by Doris Lessing

FREUD'S SELECTION OF THE OEDIPUS LEGEND AS *the* narrative of human desire has accorded special prominence to a single incest story and to a single Sophoclean prototype. Freud himself, late in life, acknowledged that the Oedipus story did not adequately represent female desire, and he rejected Jung's proposal of a female "Electra complex" precisely because it suggested too perfect a symmetry between the male and female child.[1] Emphasizing the distinctive and enduring impact of the girl's earliest pre-Oedipal relation to her mother, recent feminist psychoanalysis has extended Freud's recognition that the dynamics of female desire diverge fundamentally from those dramatized by Oedipus.[2] Feminist sociologists, moreover, have challenged the basis for the Oedipal model, because in reality incest occurs most frequently, not between the young boy and his adult mother but between the adult man and his younger daughter, who is the victim, not the agent, of incestuous desire.[3]

An alternative model of incestuous feminine desire emerges from Oedipus's daughter (and sister): Antigone. Shifting our attention to Antigone means turning away from the hierarchical parent-child relationship to the more egalitarian structure of the brother-sister bond. For this reason, and others, the story of Antigone has often captured the female literary imagination. By restoring Antigone's primacy within the

Sophoclean trilogy (where "her" play predates those of Oedipus) and reviving her story as a prototype for twentieth-century narrative by women, I seek to present a distinctively female model of incestuous attachment as political defiance.

To do this requires some redefinitions. The Antigone story is not literally about incest, nor are many fictional versions of the sister-brother bond. Yet I will argue that, for several reasons, the representation of specifically sexual desire between sister and brother is not central to the symbolic function of this story. What *is* central is a primary bond which precludes the sister's marriage and thus her role in establishing exogamy. Several factors converge to emphasize this exclusive loyalty rather than an overtly sexual attachment. First, the incestuous sibling bond is typically imagined as latently, rather than overtly, sexual, because it originates in a developmental stage at which *neither* partner is sexually experienced. The taboo on sexual explicitness in women's writing, moreover, especially in writing about a tabooed sexuality, would insure that the sexual dimension of the bond would be suggested only obliquely. Most importantly, however, the distinctive symbolic value of the brother-sister relationship does not depend on its explicit sexuality but on its role in posing an opposition between the familiar, familial object of affection and the unrelated suitor, between the bonds of nature and those of society.

For many nineteenth-century readers, the *Antigone*, not the *Oedipus*, presented the essential form of tragedy by depicting the conflict between two equally powerful and valid laws: the divine law sanctioning family ties and the human law supporting secular authority. The specific issue of the brother-sister bond does not feature prominently in nineteenth-century interpretations of the play. Yet because brother-sister intimacy recurs as such an obsessive theme in nineteenth-century literature—in William Wordsworth, Lord Byron, Percy Bysshe Shelley, Emily Brontë, George Eliot, Charles Dickens, François-René Châteaubriand, Johann Goethe, Ludwig Tieck, and Richard Wagner, to name a few—it seems plausible that the centrality of the bond between Antigone and Polynices affected at least subliminally the assessment of the play's importance. By bringing this material to the forefront of the play, I simply subject the *Antigone* to a re-interpretation analogous to that Freud performed on the *Oedipus*, when he claimed that the effect of that play "does not lie in the contrast between destiny and human will [as standard interpretations asserted], but is to be looked for in the particular nature of the material on which that contrast is exemplified...His destiny moves us only because it might have been ours...It is the fate of all of us, perhaps, to direct our first sexual impulse towards our mother and our first hatred and our first murderous wish against our father."[4] The particular nature of the material in the *Antigone*—the conflict between the sister's allegiance to her brother and her allegiance to her uncle, the king, and the son he offers to her as husband—is as central to this play as the more abstract thematic opposition between the laws of family and those of state.

Several different issues coalesce in Antigone's refusal to obey the law of Creon that no one bury her brother Polynices, who had died leading a troop of forces against Thebes. By choosing to bury Polynices, Antigone knows that she chooses her own death over her marriage to Creon's son, Haemon. Her choice is thus not only one of principle but also a personal decision to "lie with Polynices" in the "marriage chamber" of his tomb rather than to marry the man selected by the substitute for her father.[5] This marriage would transfer Antigone out of her family of birth, the doomed and disgraced House of Thebes, with which she strongly identifies, into the current ruling family of Thebes; it would integrate her simultaneously into a new family and into the state. It would also affirm the authority of Creon as king, father, and as male. One of Creon's most fundamental objections to Antigone's defiance of his law is that she, as a woman, challenges his privilege as a man. "I am no man and she the man instead/if she can have this conquest without pain." "No woman rules me while I live." "I won't be called weaker than womankind."[6] In affirming her bond with her brother, and in so doing rejecting her roles as Creon's subject and prospective daughter-in-law, Antigone is also challenging the fundamental structure of patriarchy. Yet Antigone is not acting in order to assert her rights as a woman but to assert the value of her relation to her brother. She is explicit that this relationship carries more weight for her than those of marriage and motherhood, and that it is in part *this* evaluation Creon cannot tolerate: "Had I children or their father dead,/I'd let them moulder. I should not have chosen/in such a case to cross the state's decree./ What is the law that lies behind these words?/ One husband gone, I might have found another,/or a child from a new man in first child's place,/but with my parents hid away in death,/no brother, ever, could spring up for me./ Such was the law by which I honored you./ But Creon thought the doing was a crime,/a dreadful daring, brother of my heart."[7] (It is interesting to note that Antigone does not consider whether she would bury her parents, although they are as irreplaceable as her brother, and that her omission pits the claims of the brother directly against those of husband and children.) Finally, Antigone is honoring not just the claims of family in general, but those of a very particular family—the incestuous family *par excellence*. When the Chorus suggests that Antigone may be doomed through the crime of her father, she not only agrees—implying that her own transgression may bear some relationship to his—but also goes on to suggest that the specific penalty for being the child of an incestuous union is the renunciation of marriage, the antithesis of incest: "My mother's marriage-bed./ Destruction where she lay with her husband-son,/ my father. These are my parents and I their child./ I go to stay with them. My curse is to die unwed."[8]

This very cursory reading of the *Antigone* points to certain recurrent features of the sister's version of the brother-sister bond (regardless of the gender of the author) and to certain constant differences between the sister's narrative and the brother's. These differences derive from fundamental gender asymmetries. First, brothers offer sisters a relation less unequal than the daughter's relation to her father, or to his surrogates, the central authority figures in her life. Antigone poses the unspoken claims of her brother against the absolute and autocratic claims of her uncle, who occupies the place of her father. The reverse, however, is not the case: because sons are not governed, or given in marriage, by mothers, sisters do not offer a significantly less hierarchical relationship than mothers do. It is precisely, in fact, women's social impotence that creates the distinctive coloration of the sister's incest story. As Claude Levi-Strauss has argued, the social purpose of the incest prohibition is to create cultural systems of alliance and to avoid the social fragmentation that would be produced if sisters and brothers married each other: "Incest is socially absurd before it is morally culpable. Women are the vehicle for these alliances: it is a "universal fact, that the relationship of reciprocity which is the basis of marriage is not established between men and women, but between men by means of women, who are merely the occasion of this relationship." This is the case "even when the girl's feelings are taken into consideration," because marriage is subordinate to "a wider cycle of reciprocity, which pledges the union of a man and a woman who is either someone's daughter or sister, by the union of the daughter or sister of that man or another man with the first man in question."[9] For the sister to subvert this system by refusing to be an object of exchange, and actually to invert it by choosing the very brother by whom she is to be exchanged, is to endow her choice with a profoundly antisocial valence. A brother's choice of his sister, by contrast, is simply further evidence of male privilege: she will be either socially ruined or emotionally consumed by their relationship; he will not. Because men are expected to be less sexually exclusive than women, brothers can be both exogamous and endogamous, combining marriage with extremely intimate relations with their sisters, or half-sisters, or sisters-in-law (as in their significantly different ways, William Wordsworth, Lord Byron, George and Gerald Duckworth, and Charles Dickens did).

Because in choosing sisters, brothers need not sacrifice themselves nor challenge the fundamental law of exogamy, their versions of this incest story lack the political dimension that marks the story of Antigone. Instead, the brother's version tends to display a certain Romantic individualism, a contempt for social convention, but not a deliberate challenge to it. It is geared to shock morality, not to pose questions about the fundamental law that constitutes society. The difference between the brother's and sister's choice also determines a structural feature of this narrative. It is the sister's husband or fiancé, not the brother's wife, who is the crucial third figure in the sibling incest story. Antigone chooses between Polynices and Haemon; Brontë's Catharine Earnshaw between Heathcliff and Linton; Eliot's Maggie Tulliver between Tom and Stephen; Wagner's Sieglinde between Siegfried and Hunding; Mann's Sieglinde between Siegfried and von Beckerath; Lessing's Freda between Fred and Charlie. Because a choice is not essential to the brother's attachment to his sister, the other woman is irrelevant to the narrative. Finally, the inequality of brother and sister shapes the outcome of their narratives. Sisters—like Antigone—often choose to sacrifice their lives for their brothers; or—like Maggie Tulliver or Catharine Earnshaw—they may die from the conflicts generated by allegiance to their "brother." Brothers, by contrast, do not sacrifice themselves for their sisters and may even sacrifice their sister's life or reputation or well-being in order to advance their own. "I loved her, and destroyed her," Byron's Manfred admits about Astarte. "Everything about you is just like me—and so—what you have—with Beckerath [her fiancé]—the experience—is for me too," claims Thomas Mann's Siegfried before starting to make love to his sister.[10] Faulkner's Charles Bon threatens to marry his half-sister Judith, who does not know they are related, in order to elicit his father's recognition. The sister's attachment to her brother is thus often destructive to her. But so is her status as an object of exchange. For the sister to represent her allegiance to her brother as her conscious rejection of her prescribed social function transforms a relationship that may still oppress her into a gesture of defiance. By embedding her choice in a particular narrative structure, she inscribes it as a challenge to the central social law.

Two texts by Doris Lessing help substantiate these claims. "Each Other," one of Lessing's favorite short stories, is an explicit brother-sister incest narrative, a revision of Thomas Mann's "The Blood of the Walsungs," itself a revision of Wagner's *Die Walkure*.[11] To situate this story within the large context of Lessing's concerns, I would like to look first at the incest motif in her most famous novel, *The Golden Notebook*, which is riddled with incestuous cross-currents. This novel's dominant mode of incestuous desire, recognizably Oedipal, is experienced only by male characters. The great majority of Anna's lovers—Michael, Saul, Nelson, da Silva—perceive themselves as little boys and women as their mothers; these Oedipal dynamics inevitably generate ambivalence. "Yeah, you're my mom," Nelson shouts at his wife in a miniature archetypal drama embedded in the novel, "*He* [his analyst] says so. He's always right. Well it's O.K. to hate your mom, it's in the book."[12] These dynamics are concentrated in Anna's adolescent male double, Tommy, the son of her closest friend. When Tommy finds he cannot choose a career and cannot move out of his mother's home, he attempts to kill himself but only succeeds—like Oedipus—in blinding himself. Tommy's blindness, like Oedipus's according to Freud's reading, is a substitute for castration: the punishment for the incestuous relation with the mother. And Tommy's reward for this self-inflicted punishment is *the* Freudian reward for renouncing the mother: not mother herself, but a woman *like* her—in this case, her literal replacement, the second wife his father has recently discarded.

This whole Oedipal drama is alien to Anna's own experience. Her father is totally absent from the novel, except for the brief appearance of his fictional counterpart in the yellow notebook, and her daughter similarly grows up without a father. Anna does not relate to men as a daughter. Although Lessing is not explicit about an alternative heterosexual model, she does suggest a pattern that recalls Antigone's choice. Anna finally resolves her tempestuous relationship with Saul, the last in a series of stormy relationships with men, by transforming her response to him as lover into a perception of him as brother: "I felt towards him as if he were my brother, as if, like a brother, it wouldn't matter how we strayed from each other, how far apart we were, we would always be flesh of one flesh, and think each other's thoughts" (p. 641). This identification, which empowers Anna's writing, appears the sexual telos toward which the novel works. Anna's perception of Saul as brother sets her free from her futile round of self-destructive relationships; she concludes the novel she composes from the sentence Saul gives her by describing her move to a smaller flat, where no spare room awaits a man.

Lessing offers no explanation for this brother metaphor. To understand its power for Anna, we must see it in the context of Anna's black notebook. In this narrative recording her despairing realization that the Communist effort could not transform African society, Anna's final response to Saul is prefigured by the enigmatic figure of Maryrose, the only character to challenge the increasingly apparent sterility of Communist rhetoric. The movement leadership depicted in this notebook is exclusively male. Anna is tolerated as "the leader's girlfriend," Maryrose because she is beautiful; both women are considered irrelevant to the political exchanges among the men. In the midst of this sterile atmosphere, however, Maryrose commits the only genuinely radical act: she talks about her incestuous relationship with her brother. Her repeated question, "What's wrong with that?" silences her male comrades by challenging a law far more fundamental than any they have criticized. Maryrose's brother, whom she has loved more than anyone and with whom she has had an explicitly sexual relationship, has been killed in the war. Metaphorically, Maryrose has buried her life with his by falling instantly in love with a man who resembles him and who refuses to marry her. By choosing to remain loyal to her dead brother and to his facsimile, despite (or because of) the unavailability of both, Maryrose effectively removes herself from the system of sexual exchange. Passionately courted by every heterosexual man portrayed in this notebook, Maryrose deliberately remains sexually and intellectually detached and able through her simple reiterated question to puncture the self-importance of her male peers and to voice a position more radical and more affirmative than the stilted rhetoric in which they indulge. When Anna echoes Maryrose's choice at the end of *The Golden Notebook*, she reinforces the implication that allegiance to the brother can insulate women from a political and sexual hierarchy determined by men.

"Each Other," written a few years earlier, is a far more graphic account of brother-sister incest. Lessing updates

Thomas Mann's 1905 story "The Blood of the Walsungs" by changing the setting from turn-of-the-century Germany to contemporary London and by substituting the mundane Fred and Freda for the Wagnerian Siegfried and Sieglinde. More significantly, Lessing alters the framework of the story. In "The Blood of the Walsungs," Sieglinde is engaged, not married, to the intimidated and ineffectual von Beckerath, who is "overcome by anybody asking his permission about anything."[13] The story is told almost exclusively from Siegfried's point of view; Sieglinde is merely the female counterpart to his carefully tended self. The story culminates in the sexual union of brother and sister, an act finally triggered by witnessing their operatic prototypes in Wagner's *Die Walkure*. It is Siegfried, however, who initiates the act; when Sieglinde wonders afterwards how von Beckerath will react, Siegfried implies that his motive has been in part to assert his primacy over the husband. Lessing's story reverses the sequence of events. Freda is already married, and the story opens with the husband's voice. The power structure is also different. Charlie, who has married Freda "with confidence in the manhood which had mastered her freakish adolescence," is no ineffectual suitor but a traditional patriarchal husband intent on asserting his authority.[14] Fred, by contrast, offers equality and escape from the constrictions of marriage. The point of view has thus shifted to the sister's choice, the classic structure of the female story of sister-brother incest.

Lessing's other major deviation from Mann is her audacious portrayal of the sexual relationship. In "The Blood of the Walsungs," the sexual consummation is conventionally euphemistic and elliptical: "They forgot themselves in caresses, which took the upper hand, passing over into a tumult of passion, dying away into a sobbing . . ." (p. 319). As in most representations of incest, the focus is on the unorthodox choice of object, not on the sexual experience itself. In "Each Other" Lessing attempts to envision a mode of sexuality distinctive to incest. The outstanding feature of this mode in Lessing's text is the careful avoidance of orgasm, banished by Fred and Freda to the banal sexual realm Freda shares with her husband, and Fred with his girlfriend. By systematically moving toward and avoiding climax, whispering instructions to each other only in the negative ("no," "wait," "don't"), Fred and Freda achieve a different kind of fusion "when the hungers of the flesh were held by love on the edge of fruition so long that they burned out and up and away into a flame of identity" (p. 218). Sexual desire, Lessing implies, is hungry, devouring; it creates the illusion of unity by canceling out the other. By kindling, then thwarting, this desire, Fred and Freda instead achieve a shared identity.

"Each Other" only teases us into imagining just how this happens. But in this challenge to our notions of sexuality lies the story's political significance. Unlike other sister-brother incest stories, Freda needn't finally choose between her husband and her brother; in fact, the husband is the necessary complement to the brother, the routine that enriches the variation. Rather than the antithesis to incest, marriage becomes its prerequisite. "Each Other" forces us to reconceptualize the oppositions on which our culture rests. Because the incestuous relationship in "Each Other" is not the expression of unrestrained instinctual desire, but a highly cultivated art requiring perfect self-control, the polarity between instinctual incestuous desire and the renunciations demanded by culture is forcefully called into question. Nature/culture, incest/marriage, instinct/sublimation: the story asks us to reconsider these dichotomies. In so doing, it poses as basic a challenge to our cultural assumptions as does the story of the sister who chooses brother over husband and refuses to enter the system of exchange.

Brothers and sisters use the same language of mirroring to describe their attraction to each other, and this has beguiled critics into reading their incest narratives as if they too were mirror images. There *is* no basic difference between Catharine Earnshaw's cry, "I *am* Heathcliff" and David Copperfield's claim that Agnes is "the center of myself." The difference lies not in sibling psychology but in the different social positions brother and sister hold. I know of no fraternal counterpart to the story of Antigone, no story where the brother's allegiance to his sister is also a challenge to the father and the king. At the opposite end of the spectrum, however, we might find a telling analog:

the story of Narcissus who, according to a second-century account by Pausanias, fell in love with his twin sister and embraced his own reflection, after her death, because it resembled her. Perhaps the most striking difference that gender inserts in potentially parallel incest narratives is the narcissistic cast it confers on one, the political temper it grants the other.

NOTES

1. Freud rejects the term "Electra Complex" in "Female Sexuality" (1931). For a fuller account of his position, see "Female Sexuality," "Some Psychical Consequences of the Anatomical Distinction between the Sexes" (1925), and "Femininity" (1933), conveniently collected in *Women & Analysis: Dialogues on Psychoanalytic Views of Femininity*, ed. Jean Strouse (New York: Grossman Publishers, 1974).

2. The central books in this rich field include Nancy Chodorow, *The Reproduction of Mothering: Psychoanalysis and the Sociology of Gender* (Berkeley and Los Angeles: University of California Press, 1978); Dorothy Dinnerstein, *The Mermaid and the Minotaur: Sexual Arrangements and Human Malaise* (New York: Harper & Row, 1976); and Carol Gilligan, *In a Different Voice: Psychological Theory and Women's Development* (Cambridge: Harvard University Press, 1982).

3. See esp. Judith Lewis Herman, *Father-Daughter Incest* (Cambridge: Harvard University Press, 1981).

4. Sigmund Freud, *The Interpretation of Dreams*, trans. James Strachey (New York: Avon Books, 1965), 296.

5. Sophocles, *Antigone*, trans. Elizabeth Wyckoff (Chicago: University of Chicago Press, 1954), 11. 73, 891.

6. Ibid., 11. 484-85, 525, 680.

7. Ibid., 11. 906-15.

8. Ibid., 11. 862-65

9. Claude Levi-Strauss, *The Elementary Structures of Kinship*, trans. James Harle Bell, John Richard Von Sturmer, and Rodney Needham, ed. (Boston: Beacon Press, 1969), 485, 115-16.

10. Thomas Mann, "The Blood of the Walsungs," in *Stories of Three Decades*, trans. H.T. Lowe-Porter (New York: Alfred A. Knopf, 1936), 319.

11. See Doris Lessing's interview with Roy Newquist in *A Small Personal Voice*, ed. Paul Schlueter (New York: Vintage Books, 1975), 54.

12. Doris Lessing, *The Golden Notebook* (New York: Simon & Schuster, 1962), 491. All references are to this edition; subsequent page numbers appear in parentheses in the text.

13. Mann, *Stories*, 304.

14. Doris Lessing, "Each Other," in *A Man and Two Women* (New York: Popular Library, 1963), 210.

Nicole Ward Jouve

Doris Lessing: A "Female Voice"—Past, Present, or Future?

Feminist attempts to "make" theory, to define a "female voice," female language, come up against an invisible but closed border. Sociocultural accounts of "experience" rely upon realist "representation"; they revive hierarchies, notions of authorship, of greatness. Talk about the "female body" raises the ghost of biology or the even more threatening one of "fascist-type" "discourse." Attempts to get out of the "sexual fix" produce eloquent accounts of what is bad but do not say much about that elusive infinity, "female desire." Work on myths and images has been brilliant in its analyses, or its attempts at subversion, but it too has trouble going beyond the "ideal," or the "negative."

Yet some writers do speak a "female language." Their *practice* covers the ground that theory cannot. I think as I say this of Brazilian Clarice Lispector, of French "avant-garde" writers such as Marguerite Duras, Helene Cixous, Chantal Chawaf, Jeanne Hyvrard, Christiane Veschambre, Catherine Weinzaepflen. . . .

Were I to attempt to *say* what it is they *do*, I would immediately get caught in the theoretical double bind. Let me just tentatively suggest, then, that some arguably "feminine" values emerge from their work: a sense of the self as multiple, as trans-personal, able to relate to "universal forces";[1] geared to "pre-Oedipal" depths, immersed in the substance of life;[2] seeking for an equilibrium, a state of neutrality, negativity even, with reality.[3] In their work is a strongly meditative stance, the attempt to overcome divisions, boundaries, hierarchies.

Wouldn't all this be a pretty good description of what Doris Lessing is seeking to establish in her *Canopus* series? You could even say that this is what "Canopus," that mysterious "planet," stands for. Yet how can that be? Lessing has repeatedly repudiated the "feminine" voice, stated that what women are trying to do is negligible by contrast with the magnitude of the "real" issues. Also, she never sheds her "enormous" authorial ego.[4] However diverse the narrative modes of the *Canopus* series, the author's relation to her galactic world, from the infinitely large to the infinitely small, is more like Ambien II's overview of space and time in her transparent, well-sealed bubble of a spacecraft, than a descent into the night of unknowing. In Marguerite Duras, a void, an absence, are the means to reach multitudes, through multiple years. *Les Mains Negatives* are the outline of hands on rocks by the sea, drawn red or blue in prehistoric time: they become a cry of love, screamed thirty thousand years ago, heard only by those who scream that same scream by the sea. In *Le Navire Night*, a man and a woman find each other through a chance call in the sea of calls of the telephone exchange. They live an intense passion. They never meet. "People who scream in the night in the abyss make assignations. The assignations never lead to encounters. Enough that they should be made."[5]

If you contrast this with the appointments, steadily followed by encounters, between Ambien II and Klorathy in *The Syrian Experiments*, you immediately see what "realistic" control Doris Lessing keeps over her world. The meetings may be nominally from millennia to millennia and through light-years, but they are as solid, make you as little dizzy, as if they were at the cafe round the corner. And all the time, Ambien II is supposed to be unlearning control, slowly entering the realm of unknowing.

And yet . . . coming across names like "Ambien" (suggesting ambivalence, a kind of androgyny, as well as ambience, atmospheric communication)—characters like Nasar who in his successive lives can be alternatively male and female—I am reminded of Catherine Weinzaepflen's *La Parole Nomade* which hovers round gender; you never know whether the two correspondents whose letters make up the book are male or female. Similarly, confronted with the "choric" or shifting chroniclers of *The Marriages between Zones Three, Four, and Five* or of *The Making of the Representative for Planet 8*, I think of Helene Cixous's *With ou l'art de l'innocence*, where the writer attempts to be "like a fish in writing." Multiple personae, coauthors, Aura, Antouilya, Amina, Amyriam, surround, and dialogue with, H. (Helene); together they make the shoal of the sea-text. I think, that is, that, especially in *The Marriages*—Doris Lessing may be trying to make "authoriality" diffuse, multiple, transpersonal. One of the Chroniclers there, after all, does say that he becomes what he describes: "I am Ben Ata when I summon him into my mind."[6] A "*golden*" folktale, or myth, tries to come into being, in which the *four* Zones are de-partitioned, made to flow into each other. And instead of the author of a "*notebook*" you have multiple authors, inhabited by voices, and they all in turn mean to affect the reader, who is to be part of the "we." Al.Ith's descent into Zone Four is "for us all" (pp. 176-77).[7] The (Sufi?) fable extends its teaching to the reader. The text, you could say, is "writerly" in that the reader needs actively to participate in its making for it to "happen."

Is that truly so?

Take Vahshi, the Queen of Zone Five. She stands for all sorts of primitivism. She is wild, anarchic, vital, sensation-based, unself-conscious. You could say that she stands for the "pre-Oedipal." And yet, when you come to think about it, you realize that you assume this because you are *told* that it is so, not because the writing itself, as writing, gives evidence of this. Vahshi's soldiers (like Germanic Barbarians looking at the Roman-type soldiery of Zone Four) are described as follows: "her desert men skirmished about, communicating in wild yells and shrieks their surprise and dislike of this safe, domestic and tame little kingdom . . . [they] added to the ferment and the danger" (p. 295). Ben Ata says of Vahshi that "she argues for unrestrained freedom in all things—license, anarchy" (p. 292). When she herself is shown thinking, she does it in indirect free speech. "Oh no, she was not sorry that Ben Ata had gone. She was glad—he had been a weight, a heaviness. . . . She longed for one thing: that she could go back to being as she had been before [she knew] . . . that one could think" (p. 266).

Does this sound to you like a "pre-Oedipal" or anarchic self in its first tottering steps toward thinking? Shouldn't Vahshi sound more like Kaspar Hauser and less like a nineteenth-century heroine? Contrast with this:

> Ma voix veut vivre dans une langue prehistorique, en les regions non cadastrees. Je veux mots nument, syllabes, nomades, pre-non-fixes, mots regorgeant de mots, coquillages, faune, pactive, pas si passive, assise,
>
> Je veux languelait, qu'est-ce qu'il y a dans l'anglais,
>
> L'en, il y a l'en, il y a lent, et l'angle, je veux l'englaise, langue sans angoisse
>
> le gaie langue . . .
>
> . . .
>
> Kennst du das Langue wo die Zitronen zungen?[29]
>
> (My voice wants to live in a prehistoric language, in unchartered regions. I want naked words (moan you meant /monument/mots nument), syllables, nomadic, pre-non-fixed, words overflowing with words, shells, faun, pactive, not so passive, so sat,
>
> I want tongue-milk (English), what is there in English,
>
> In, there is In, Ing, and angle, I want the In-clay, language without anguish,
>
> the gay language . . .
>
> . . .
>
> Kennst du das Langue wo die Zitronen zungen?)

In this passage by Helene Cixous, language becomes the Koh-*i*-Noor: in the middle of the diamond, an "i" glitters. Anarchy is actualized by the proliferating and shifting and sensuous language. The sounds play, resonate. A ferment is set to work, like the "i" in the middle of the name "Koh-*i*-Noor." In the Doris Lessing, you are *told* that the desert men are a ferment. You do not experience it.

The same could be said about Al.Ith's mystical entry into Zone II, though there, as in moments of *The Making* Lessing gets a bit closer to the state she wishes to adumbrate. The name of the character does suggest alternatives. Al.Ith. Alice? with a lilt, and a childish lisp. I-Is. Alice into the blue of Zone Two: through the looking glass? The punctuation mark at the center displaces a normal sense of "period." The "dash" is rounded, like Wittig's "O" in *Les Guerilleres*. Also, Arabic "Al" ("El"—"La" in reverse) versus Arabic "Ben" (Ata) and Hindu-sounding Vahshi. The names, that is, have a multifarious, across-the-borders glitter. They are not far away from Cixous's Antouilya and Amyriam. But the glitter stops at the names. Al.Ith's voyage into blueness never alters the basic laws of naming, the structures of syntax, the "specious plausibility" of the "historical" mode.

> What she had seen was blue, always blue, distances speaking in colour, but now she expected to see closeness dissolve the blue. And yet it did not. . . . And her mind was not as clear as it could be, and as she relied on it to be. . . . She was struggling through a thick blue air which her lungs were labouring to use. It was like milk dyed with blue, or like . . . air was not far off a liquid. . . . (Pp. 236-37)

Suspension marks is as far as the disruption goes. We are "told" and shown through external events (the death of the horse, etc.) that Al.Ith has entered a process of "depersonalization," and we are made to feel that it is a superior kind of state. But we do not know what the state is, what it actually means, because the prose does not create it. The contrast is strong with Clarice Lispector, whose *Passion According to G.H.* is about "depersonalization." The book is a poetic meditation, wave upon wave, that goes ever deeper into contemplation of the ordinary—the unclean—disgust—through utter disgust—into acceptance, love—and beyond that, neutrality. The book communicates an extraordinarily immediate sense of what being spiritually stripped *means*.

Yet—despite my ill-concealed doubts and preferences—it remains true that the writers I have mentioned and Lessing have much in common. The stance of the Chroniclers of Zone Three, the values represented by Zone Five and Zone Two, and the need to open out to them are what "writerly" women writers create as a "feminine" utterance. It has to be "written," to be "uttered," because it is somehow "ahead," a mode of being to be desired. Writing gives form and status to what has no currency. The modes of being which Duras and Lispector shadow forth, the "gay language" beyond separate languages, in which the lemon trees would flower, which Helene Cixous dreams of, are as much ahead of us in their way as the paradisal state of affairs among the Zones at the end of Lessing's novel. Interesting to note, though, that paradise, for women, seems to be ahead, not lost. That innocence is an art to be learned, like Canopus's responsiveness to "Need": not something "experience" has estranged us from.

And so, the "writerly texts" do not go seeking for past time, are not concerned with origins, reporting. There is no story to see you through. The dominant mode is the present, a present open to the flow, the overflowing, the care for a future which only the vibrant openness, the willingness to go beyond knowledge, will make possible. Sadly, this marks them out as "difficult." Their readership is yet to come, *in the future* as it were. While reading occurs, they make us into the kind of people we should become. Lessing does the reverse. She has given up on the present (which she hardly ever used as a mode, anyway) and deliberately moved into a hypothetical future, the future of "science fiction." Whether this is on account of an overwhelming sense of our ending, or because, feeling that she had exhausted the fictional possibilities of "here and now," she needed to treat herself to a clean slate, is too intricate a question to consider now. What is certain is that the most absent dimension of her Canopus series is the present. Indeed, for her future, she posits a future yet further ahead so that she can use the narrative preterit, keep to the "historical" mode. And this makes her texts easy, or relatively so—accessible, certainly. Her readers read about what they ought to become—what lies ahead of them, what they should strive to be and understand—as if it was *behind* them. Does that mean that Lessing leaves us with the shadows on the walls of the cave? Instead of turning our eyes toward the source of light? Should we instead wonder at the importance which the "yet to come," the "future," the "hypothetical," play in these diverse modes of writing and ask what it means that femininity, somehow, should seem to remain our shadowy border?

NOTES

1. Helene Cixous's *Vivre L'orange* and Jeanne Hyvrard's *Le Corps defunt la comedie* speak the body in the same breath as the "political."

2. See esp. Chantal Chawaf (*Retable: La reverie, La Cercoeur*, etc.) and Christiane Veschambre's *Le Lais de la traverse.*

3. This is seen, for example, in some Marguerite Duras, and in *Isocelles* and *Portrait et un reve* by Catherine Weinzaepflen.

4. Jean McCrindle's word, as in Jenny Taylor, ed., *Notebooks/ Memoirs/Archives: Reading and Re-reading Doris Lessing*. (Boston: Routledge & Kegan Paul, 1982), 47.

5. Marguerite Duras, *Le Navire—Cesaree—Les mains negatives —Aurelia Steiner—Aurelia Steiner—Aurelia Steiner—Aurelia Steiner* (Paris: Mercure de France, 1982), 42.

6. Doris Lessing, *The Marriages between Zones Three, Four and Five* (St. Albans, England: Panther, 1981) 242-43. All references are to this edition; subsequent references appear in parentheses in text.

7. "When these women strove and struggled to lift their poor heads up so they could see our mountains towering over them it was as if they were secretly pouring energy and effort into springs that fed us all. When Al.Ith made her forced descent to that dreary land it was for us all."

8. See Marsha Rowe's interesting discussion on this, in *Notebooks/Memoirs/Archives*, " 'If you mate a Swan and a Gander, who will Ride?' " 191-205.

9. Helene Cixous, *With ou l'art de l'innocence* (Paris: Edition femmes, 1981), 302-303. (Note: there is among others a pun on "monument," the stately French language having been compared to one. "Mots nument" suggests "words nakedly." I tried to render the pun as "moan you meant," but Anthony Ward has suggested to me you could instead translate "monument" as "edifice," and "mots nument" as "I deface").

VICTORIA MIDDLETON

Doris Lessing's "Debt" to Olive Schreiner

IF SHE WERE ALIVE IN THE 1980S, OLIVE SCHREINER would read Doris Lessing with admiration and a sense of *deja vu*. Lessing's vision is in part made possible, as she has generously admitted, by what Olive Schreiner saw in their native land of southern Africa. Both writers were raised in strict colonialist families, as Lorna Sage points out in her study of Lessing's African fiction.[1] Both educated themselves after attending schools they found stifling and condescending to women. Both moved to the more intellectually stimulating atmosphere of London, where they were sustained in exile by memories of the African landscape. They studied the most avant-garde psychological and political theories of their times, but their vision owes less to doctrine than to a transcendental perception of the natural world. Although they express their idealism in necessarily different idioms, their affinities are often striking. In *The Story of an African Farm*, to which Lessing wrote a semiautobiographical introduction, Schreiner exalts "the Divine compensation of Nature": "It is as though our mother smoothed our hair, and we are comforted."[2] In *Shikasta* (1979), Lessing describes a sense of cosmic unity as a "soft singing wind that clears our sad muddled minds and holds us safe and heals us and feeds us with lessons we never imagined."[3]

The universe that Lessing has created in her recent space fiction evolves from her early fascination with the African landscape. Like Olive Schreiner, Doris Lessing found in Africa a sustaining home for the individual spirit. Also like Schreiner, Lessing expresses despair that human beings cannot overcome their weaknesses. Their anger and frustration at society's injustices are alleviated by the possibilities for wonder that Africa continually affords them in imagination and revery. When showing the tiny stature and temporal insignificance of the individual relative to the natural and supernatural order, Lessing resembles Schreiner, whose landscape is a monumental, prehistoric space that dwarfs the follies and vices of the human society scrambling to survive on it. Characters like Lyndall and Waldo, and others like Mary Turner and Martha Quest, paradoxically find consolation and order in the natural world *because* it seems so indifferent and powerful in contrast to their lives.[4] Both Schreiner and Lessing draw on the power that Africa's terrain exercises over the imagination to redefine reality in their fiction.

Writers in Africa who are white and middle-class and consequently members of a ruling political establishment have often found themselves alienated from their own privileged society and drawn to what is different in the native African culture, realizing that they can never be *of* it.[5] Within the patriarchal white society, women writers may have a further experience of difference, an intensified alienation. Schreiner and Lessing show that the social sphere encourages immanence, introspection, self-doubt, and despair in women, or perhaps even worse, a false sense of liberation and privilege. It is, we may say, the "horror" or metaphysical mystery which writers like Conrad and Greene have discovered in Africa that Schreiner and Lessing regard as a vast potential space in which to imagine a life that is free of racial, sexual, and economic injustice.

Being white women and intellectuals in Africa contributes to their creative power but also to their despair. As relatively new settlers in a still open country, they are energized by dreams of action that their female contemporaries in older countries do not share. Yet as artists they must create, however unwillingly, out of a tradition, and they inherit the patriarchal literature of Western Europe. In Lessing's introduction to *The*

Story of an African Farm, she lays emphasis on Schreiner's reading: "before she was twenty [she] had read Darwin and Spencer, Montaigne, Goethe, Carlyle, Gibbon, Locke, and Lecky; J.S. Mill, Shakespeare, Ruskin, and Schiller" (p. 11). In "The Small Personal Voice," Lessing identifies her own influences: "For me, the highest point of literature was the novel of the nineteenth century, the work of Tolstoy, Stendhal, Dostoevsky, Balzac, Turgenev, Chekhov; the work of the great realists."[6] For this reason, perhaps, both Lessing and Schreiner had to be writers in England, to come to terms with the culture which gave them language to "create" their own Africa but which also inscribed them as white women in a series of plots that diminished their potential.

The predicament of the white woman in the African landscape is the subject of Olive Schreiner's *The Story of an African Farm* (1883) and Doris Lessing's *The Grass Is Singing* (1959), as well as Lessing's *African Stories*[7] and much of her *Children of Violence* series. The heroines of these books—Lyndall, Mary Turner, and Martha Quest—struggle for self-definition in a capitalistic, racist society that cherishes the beautiful white girl as one of its most valuable commodities. In *The Story of an African Farm*, Lyndall eloquently criticizes the invisible, silken bonds that tie women down.

> We go and stand before the glass. We see the complexion we were not to spoil, and the white frock, and we look into our own great eyes. Then the curse begins to act on us. It finishes its work when we are grown women, who no more look wistfully at a more healthy life; we are contented. We fit our sphere as a Chinese woman's foot fits her shoe, exactly, as though God had made both—and yet He knows nothing of either. In some of us the shaping to our end has been quite completed. The parts we are not to use have been quite atrophied, and have been dropped off; but in others, and we are not less to be pitied, they have been weakened and left. We wear the bandages, but our limbs have not grown to them; we know that we are compressed, and chafe against them. (p. 176).

Drawing on her reading (as the reference to Chinese footbinding would suggest) and not her observation of barefoot African women, Lyndall denounces the condition of all women who must passively "seem" while men act (p. 175). Women's only work is to attract men; their power, as J.S. Mill explained, is desperate and manipulative because it is unauthorized (p. 177, p. 179). Their domestic labor as mothers and wives is devalued, and as unmarried women, they are worthless (pp. 180-82).

Lyndall's list of grievances describe Mary Turner in *The Grass Is Singing*. The image of the white woman as a cherished luxury or valuable prize dupes her into marrying, just as it dupes Dick Turner, who is enchanted by her image in the false light of a movie theater. Mary's murder results from her ignorance of herself, which can be traced to her miserable family background, her conventional education, her false sense of liberation as a working girl in the city. "South Africa is a wonderful place: for the unmarried white woman," Lessing notes ironically (p. 34). Mary's lack of self-knowledge is matched by her total incomprehension of the land and the native workers. She tries frantically to "pu(t) things to right" in the wretched house, as if embroidering and whitewashing will keep her from being alone with herself (p. 64). She is hardly a "person on her own account" but merely the victim of psycho-political circumstances (p. 35). White women such as Mary are actually like the native African women they despise. As Lessing writes of the displaced native woman in *Going Home*, "this woman comes into town, and she is nothing. She is nothing. She is only a wife, only a mother. All her other roles have gone."[8] Women of both races are rendered powerless and superfluous by their exploitative society, which regards them as either ornamental objects or as instruments of labor.

Schreiner and Lessing emphasize the dehumanizing consequences of capitalism and the class system for men as well as women. In *The Story of an African Farm*, Waldo angrily rejects the indifference and brutality he meets while working as a clerk in town. In *The Grass Is Singing*, Dick Turner's repeated failures as a farmer and Charlie Slatter's success indict the abusive treatment of the African soil and its people that increases wealth but exhausts and destroys life. Failures populate Lessing's African stories such as "Eldorado" and "The Second Hut," in which ordinary men are undone by the country they hoped to master and profit from.

In this competitive society, men and women find little peace together. In *The Story of an African Farm*, Lyndall's primary friendship is with the feminine Waldo, who labors to give birth to a sheep-shearing machine, the child of his imagination, which is destroyed as is Lyndall's baby. Lyndall cannot safely have an intimate relationship with her mysterious lover, for the erotic plot he acts in requires the loss of her independence (pp. 223-25). And Gregory Rose is deluded by romantic notions, until he dons women's clothes and experiences his own "womanhood," nursing Lyndall on her deathbed. There can be no satisfying heterosexual relationships combining "friendship, passion, worship," Schreiner suggests, until the fundamental plots of desire and mutual destruction that are concealed in the social comedy of realism are rewritten (p. 216).

Schreiner said "she had put herself" into both Waldo and Lyndall, as Lessing observes in her introduction (pp. 6-7). Doris Lessing similarly sympathizes with women but envies men's freedom and vision. She shows ironic sympathy for the white women's pathetic civilizing impulses in her *African Stories*, in "The De Wets Come to Kloof Grange," "Little Tembi," and "Flavours of Exile." In "Old John's Place," "Getting Off the Altitude," and "Lucy Grange," she analyzes the unhappy passion of idle, lonely women transplanted to the veld. On the other hand, Lessing empathizes with Johnny Blakeworth in "The Story of a Non-Marrying Man." He prefers tribal life to the "suffocating" domesticity of marriage to an Englishwoman, even several women (p. 649). He gets free of the conventionality and brutalizing materialism of town life when he escapes to live with a native tribe.

Lessing's sympathy in *The Grass Is Singing* is carefully diffused and distanced. Mary's murder seems like the punishing of a victim. But Lessing uses biblical parallels—Moses is her judge and executioner—and allusions to *The Waste Land* to underscore why it is the woman who is destroyed in this patriarchal tragedy. Mary's death is the inevitable outcome of the way she is written into the conventional marriage plot. To the end, Mary remains uncomprehending—"Against what had she sinned?"—but accepting that she has violated her personal relationship with Moses confers on her a "queerly appropriate dignity," a measure of humanity that white society did not foster in her (p. 230, p. 237).

Small successes appear radical victories in these conditions. In Schreiner's novel, Waldo's nurturing personality (he is humorously compared to an old hen) and Lyndall's ambition are less surprising than Gregory Rose's conversion to "womanhood." Like Mary Turner, and with as little comprehension, Gregory Rose experiences the breakdown of his conventional ideas about gender and power. In the process, he discovers a better self.

The authors' vision extends far beyond their characters': Lessing and Schreiner see past the crowded space, the troubled middle distance of sexual and racial and economic domination, by recreating the innocent wonder and ardor of a child's discovery of the physical universe. Schreiner's epigraph to *The Story of an African Farm*, taken from Alexis de Tocqueville, implies that society warps the potential of human beings.

> We must see the first images which the external world casts upon the dark mirror of his mind; or must hear the first words which awaken the sleeping powers of thought, and stand by his earliest efforts, if we would understand the prejudices, the habits, and the passions that will rule his life. The entire man is, so to speak, to be found in the cradle of the child.[9]

As Lyndall complains to Waldo, "We all enter the world little plastic beings, with so much natural force, perhaps, but for the rest—blank; and the world tells us what we are to be, and shapes us by the end it sets before us" (p. 175). Lyndall's pessimism is not the last word, however. Recapturing the child's primal receptivity to the universe is what both Schreiner and Lessing set against social conditioning.

Projecting themselves into the characters of Waldo and

other Wordsworthian boys, Schreiner and Lessing convey a child's optimism about creating his or her life. Like the Romantic poets, Waldo in *The Story of an African Farm* and the boy in Lessing's story "A Sunrise on the Veld" rejoice in the natural world and feel their powers expand. Before his death, although disappointed by his fruitless quest and Lyndall's death, Waldo regains a feeling of being at home in the universe.

> Waldo, as he sat with his knees drawn up to his chin and his arms folded on them, looked at it all and smiled. An evil world, a deceitful, treacherous, mirage-like world, it might be; but a lovely world for all that, and to sit there gloating in the sunlight was perfect. It was worth having been a little child, and having cried and prayed, so one might sit there. He moved his hands as though he were washing them in the sunshine. There will always be something worth living for while there are shimmery afternoons. (Pp. 284-85)

His peace will be disrupted by some new disappointment, and Schreiner goes on, "Well to die then; for, if you live, so surely as the years come, so surely as the spring succeeds the winter, so surely will passions arise" (p. 286). Still, for a moment, the individual capable of wise passiveness can know the "Divine compensation of Nature" (p. 285).

Lessing does not share Shreiner's positivistic faith in the progress of humanity or rejoice so wholly in nature's continuing despite the loss of a single individual. Her post-Romantic, post-war, post-Marxist consciousness makes her skeptical of evolutionary paradigms. There is, nevertheless, a romantic and apocalyptic strain in her portrayal of the physical universe, from the African landscape to the "Canopus in Argos" zones.

Like the nomadic pioneers and settlers in her African stories, Lessing "love(s) Africa for its own sake, and for what is best in it: its emptiness, its promise. It is still uncreated," as she says in *Going Home* (p. 10). Africa embodies unformed energies, the strong, clear contraries that are, for Lessing, the poles of existence between which an individual's imaginative and emotional responses take place. In *Going Home*, Lessing contrasts "the cycle of hot, strong light, of full, strong dark" and the empty, "scarifying barren beauty" of the African terrain with the "seethe and burden of Europe," "endless miles of heavy, damp, dead building on a dead, sour earth, inhabited by pale, misshapen, sunless creatures under a low sky of grey vapor" (pp. 8-9). A person so utterly conventional as Mary Turner in *The Grass Is Singing*, who is "nothing if not a social being," cannot survive the test of her spirit that comes in living isolated on the veld (p. 41). She fears the power of the sun and the vegetation to overrun human attempts to build something on the land. Mary has a notion of home that Lessing rejects as fraudulent: "For Mary, the word 'Home' spoken nostalgically, meant England, although both her parents were South Africans and had never been to England" (p. 29). She denies the creative and destructive power of Africa. Despite this conditioned insensitivity, even Mary can be changed. On the morning of her death, she feels "this marvelous moment of peace and forgiveness," "this wonderful rooted joy" because "the world was a miracle of color, and all for her, all for her!" (pp. 226-27).

In *Going Home*, Lessing responds to the vastness of the African veld, imaginatively rebuilding the family house from memory (p. 45). Standing in the bush under the Southern Cross, all barriers between herself and the land having fallen, she is "able to return to that other home," "and if I had had to fly back to England the next day, I would have been given what I had gone home for" (p. 31).

With comparable reverence, Schreiner describes, in *The Story of an African Farm*, the etherealizing power of the moon's "weird and . . . almost oppressive beauty" and the antithetical clarity of the "fierce sunlight" (p. 21, p. 24). She mocks the unethereal, fat Boer woman Tant' Sannie who dreams of sheep's trotters by moonlight and damns the hot weather by day. The violence and peace, monotony and beauty, of the natural world dwarf what is bad in human society but also inspire the individual imagination to realize its visions.

For Waldo, the sea becomes a symbol of humanity's search for truth.

> Only the sea is like a human being; the sky is not, nor the earth. But the sea is always moving, always something deep in itself is stirring it. It never rests; it is always wanting, wanting, wanting. It hurries on; and then it creeps back slowly without having reached, moaning. It is always asking a question, and it never gets an answer. (p. 246)

The ceaseless change that destroys individuals and their works must be accepted, however painful. For Schreiner and Lessing, it is the effort to survive and pursue the truth that redeems human suffering. In the story "The Sun between Their Feet," from *African Stories*, Lessing's narrator imagines the countryside existing in the days of the Mashona and Matabele, and in the days of the Bushmen, just as at the moment of her exploration. She watches beetles laboring to roll a ball of dung up a "mountain," following an instinct to reproduce, and silently derives a Sisyphean lesson about persistence and creativity in the face of defeat (p. 593, p. 598). In "A Sunrise on the Veld," Lessing portrays the violence in the natural world as ants devour a wounded deer and a boy learns about random, senseless human violence, and its repercussions: "There was something he had to think out. The death of that small animal was a thing that concerned him, and he was by no means finished with it" (p. 66). A true understanding of humanity's capacity for creation but also destruction comes in solitude, in the natural world. In society, power is an insidiously destructive force, more dangerous because it is concealed in the civilized structures, like the flimsy, decaying houses on the veld, intended to "protect" people from nature.

Recognizing the superior power of the world outside human society, experiencing it with awe and dread, restores a right perspective on the individual's relation to the collective. The awareness of "gigantic forces," as Lessing calls them in her introduction to Schreiner's novel, is also the potential source of human salvation (p. 6). Death simply means the individual's absorption into the cosmos. Lyndall and Waldo are, like Wordsworth's Lucy, "rolled round in earth's diurnal course." For both writers, an emotional or suprarational response to the power of the universe can redeem human beings from despair and save them from the cycles of oppression, violence, and ignorance that make up history.

Although the social world is unsatisfactory, it resembles the world of nature in that values associated with sex, race, and class are transitory and as changeable as the African light. The representation of gender and nature in Schreiner's and Lessing's fiction suggests that they believe that interchange of state is a positive, not simply a destructive process. This openness extends to their technique, for each resists adhering to a single form or style that might limit her expressiveness.

In the introduction to *African Stories*, Lessing rejects the "feminine" style of fiction that is self-conscious and mannered in favor of a straightforward, dramatic, "masculine" style that looks directly at the world (p. 8). Similarly, Schreiner worries whether her book *From Man to Man* (about the sexual and romantic trouble of two sisters) is too "womanly." In a letter to Havelock Ellis, Schreiner distinguishes between the two styles, "plain" and "ribbed," in which the book is written: "Sometimes the plain is right, sometimes the ribbed. I *think* I generally write descriptions in the plain and philosophise or paint thought in the ribbed. (You know in knitting there are two stitches: one makes a plain surface and the other makes ribs. Ribbed knitting goes up and down, up and down)."[10] She criticizes the single-mindedness of artificial, overly planned writing in favor of "organic" art that evolves naturally and inevitably (quoted by Lessing, in her introduction to *The Story of an African Farm*, pp. 3-4).

Similarly, from the first, Doris Lessing has regarded the novel as an elastic genre. In "The Small Personal Voice," she says that realism is "art which springs so vigorously and naturally from a strongly held, though not necessarily intellectually defined, view of life that it absorbs symbolism" (p. 4). Lessing admires its values—"the warmth, the compassion, the humanity, the love of people"—but she has always mingled realism and myth or fable to represent her vision of human consciousness and its relationship with the collective. Both Lessing and

Schreiner see the inadequacies of realism. It asks us to laugh at Tant' Sannie, for example, to relieve our contempt and dislike for her cruelty. But both writers are consistently faithful to the humanistic spirit that underlies realism, even as they continually seek new expression for that spirit. They use what is best in the novel tradition, expose its limitations, and seek other forms.

Their fiction owes as much to its African provenance as it does to European novels. Both women share a perspective on the isolated enclaves of settlers who transplanted themselves to Africa and attempted to translate their culture. Perhaps it was the very combination of emotional discord and spiritual peace each found on the veld that energized her creativity.

In following Schreiner, Lessing shows none of the aggressive rivalry that Harold Bloom ascribes to male poets who compete with their precursors. Lessing's view of the literary tradition is perhaps that it sustains her and offers an intellectual home. Schreiner is, of course, only one precursor, and one influence among many, including social conventions, political structures, ideologies, and landscapes.

Recognizing her affinity with Schreiner, however, perhaps means a kind of self-discovery for Lessing. In her introduction to *The Story of an African Farm*, she speculates on the psychology of the woman writer.

> To the creation of a woman novelist seems to go certain psychological ingredients; at least, often enough to make it interesting. One of them, a balance between father and mother where the practicality, the ordinary sense, cleverness, and worldly ambition is on the side of the mother; and the father's life is so weighted with dreams and ideas and imaginings that their joint life gets lost in what looks like a hopeless muddle and failure, but which holds a potentiality for something that must be recognized as better, on a different level, than what ordinary sense or cleverness can begin to conceive. (p. 9)

Lessing might be talking of herself. In the essay, "My Father," in *A Small Personal Voice*, she writes that he "could be described as uncritically superstitious or as psychically gifted" (p. 88); he was a dreamer who mused, " 'Makes you think—there are so many worlds up there, wouldn't really matter if we did blow ourselves up—plenty more where we came from' " (p. 93). This quotation appears as the epigraph to *Shikasta*, suggesting that the belief in many possible worlds that we can dream of and even perhaps bring into being may be something Lessing inherited from her father. But her legacy from Olive Schreiner, which is not felt as a debt, is the need and the means to order her African experience. Schreiner was a pioneering example of a woman writer who strove to comprehend the tragedy of history and yet cherish the natural world in which it is enacted. Both women write closely and truthfully of their respective historical moments, but their like-mindedness is not time-bound.

NOTES

1. Lorna Sage, *Doris Lessing* (New York: Methuen, 1983), 22.

2. Olive Schreiner, *The Story of an African Farm*, with an introduction by Doris Lessing (New York: Schocken, 1976), 285. All references are to this edition, unless otherwise noted; subsequent references appear in parentheses in the text.

3. Doris Lessing, *Re: Colonized Planet 5: Shikasta* (New York: Vintage, 1979), 364.

4. Sage discusses Lessing's ironic relief that Africa remains " 'still, thank God, impersonal and indifferent to man' " p. 17.

5. See Sage, *Lessing*, 21-22; and Michael Thorpe, *Doris Lessing's Africa* (New York: Africana Publishing Co., 1978), 104. Both Sage and Thorpe focus on what may be called the political uses of Africa in Lessing's work.

6. Doris Lessing, "The Small Personal Voice," in *A Small Personal Voice*, ed. Paul Schlueter (New York: Vintage, 1975), 4. All references are to this edition; subsequent references appear in parentheses in the text.

7. Doris Lessing, *The Grass Is Singing* (New York: New American Library, 1950), and *African Stories* (New York: Simon & Schuster, 1981). All references are to these editions; subsequent references appear in parentheses in the text.

8. Doris Lessing, *Going Home* (New York: Popular Library, 1957). All references are to this edition; subsequent references appear in parentheses in the text.

9. Olive Schreiner, *The Story of an African Farm* (New York: Penguin, 1971), 3.

10. Olive Schreiner, "A Note on the Genesis of the Book," *From Man to Man* (Chicago: Academy Press, 1977), xi.

CAREY KAPLAN

Britain's Imperialist Past in Doris Lessing's Futuristic Fiction

DORIS LESSING'S RECENT SPACE FICTION, FIVE RElentlessly impersonal, abstract, and instructional novels, the *Canopus in Argos* series, purports to prophesy about the future while urging readers to evolve in the direction of their full potential. Despite this futuristic and progressive message and the intergalactic setting in which the action occurs, the new series is, like all Lessing's fiction, autobiographical; in this case, it looks resolutely backwards into Britain's imperialist past, Lessing's Rhodesian cradle, for models of ideal behavior and of obedient resignation to superior beings from higher civilizations. These space fictions (and the Jane Somers books, in a different way) are depersonalized chronicles of the process of aging as experienced by a great novelist unwilling to go gentle into any good night at all, trying to wrest cosmic order and some assurance of immortality out of the raw materials and structures of her long life. Frustrated by failing powers, fading physical beauty, and the brevity of life—and fighting for resignation to the inevitable—Lessing creates an ideal world in the Canopus books in which aging and death are irrelevant to the superior colonizing beings.

Because of the trappings of modernity and futurity, physics and genetics, and because of many readers' confusion over Lessing's break with realism, the basic pattern of the Canopus books is elusive. In this discussion, I would like, as it were, to gain a Canopean perspective on the *Canopus in Argos* series: to stand, that is, at so great a distance from the works that their primary patterns emerge clearly.

The underlying template of the Canopus books can be traced back to our own past, to the British Empire and especially to Doris Lessing's own personal past as an English colonist growing up in a country clearly not "home," which cheerfully practiced apartheid. Canopus easily transposes into a benevolent version of the British imperialism that formed Lessing's early consciousness and perceptions of the world: the various planets under its umbrella and colonies full of imperfect, uncivilized, less than fully human natives, profoundly in need of the technology and wisdom of the master race. Indeed, given this context, J. Hillis Miller's dictum, that "the writing of a novel . . . is a gesture, . . . [bringing] into visibility what its author is,"[1] is possibly even more true of Lessing than of most authors. As Rebecca O'Rourke has observed, in *Canopus in Argos*, "colonization is a subject writ large—the African experience [of Lessing's youth] becomes a mirror for the universe."[2] Confirming O'Rourke's notion and amplifying its meaning, Lessing, writing about white African literature, says it is typified by a "nostalgia, a hunger, a reaching out for something lost . . . an unappeasable hunger for what is out of reach." Such writing is, she continues, "the literature of exile," expressing "the unease of those forced to divide themselves between two cultures and pay allegiance to both."[3] Although this description precisely defines most of the characters in the Canopus novels, Nicole Ward Jouve reminds readers that this division and sense of exile from both the motherland and the adopted country are basic to Lessing's earlier *oeuvre* as well: "One must return to it—to Martha-Doris Lessing having been *born* uprooted, to her 'world view' springing directly from the white settler's situation."[4] Because the colonist's rootlessness and sense of separation have been a staple of Lessing's work, the reader is not surprised to find the Canopean dramatis personae in the same existential dilemma. One immediately thinks of the divided nostalgic longing that permeates all the main characters, the sense of exile they all share. There is Johor in *Shikasta* yearning, on the one hand, for degenerated Rohanda, despoiled by Sirius, Shammat, and various cosmic accidents —very like Africa despoiled by ignorant colonization—and, on the other hand, longing for the perfections of the seat of empire, Canopus; Al.Ith in *The Marriages between Zones Three, Four, and Five* agonizingly pulled apart between desire for the unimaginable spiritual perfections of Zone Two and her love for Ben Ata in flawed and physical Zone Four; Ambien in *The Sirian Experiments* aspiring toward Canopus but mired in and loyal to Sirius, from which she is ultimately exiled; Doeg in *The Making of the Representative for Planet 8*, torn between his impulse and the need to attain a rarefied Canopean perspective and his love for his earthly, ignorant, doomed Planet 8; and Klorathy in *The Sentimental Agents*, loyal to the ideals and purposes of the Canopean Empire and the Necessity but continually seduced by the rhetoric, the emotions, and the physicality of the Volyens. Character after character in these novels exists in a never-never land, torn between aspiration to higher realms and yearning for base but desirable warm, animal contact. These are only a few of the obvious examples; the triangle of an individual powerfully attracted by two compelling but incompatible desires multiplies and echoes throughout Lessing's work. That is, the key character in many of Lessing's novels and stories, perpetually an outsider,[5] belonging to neither of the worlds for which she or he longs, wishes with the baser part of her or his nature for what is fleshly, personal, sensual, emotional, haphazard, irrational, spontaneous, and messy (in conventional iconography: female). Despite this yearning and in the midst of it, the Outsider rejects this sphere and fixes her or his sights on what is (often grudgingly and painfully) acknowledged as a higher ideal, from which the Outsider is equally estranged: that which is disembodied, impersonal, pure, reasonable, rational, unemotional, rigorous, stiff-upper-lipped, orderly, Right (and stereotypically male)—a twentieth-century version of Swift's Houyhnhnms but lacking even a hint of potential irony and with no suggestion that the Outsider is one with the Yahoos. The avatar of this triangle may be Doris Lessing herself, the Outsider, Everywoman on the veld, with the wise, omnipotent, unattainable, remote British Empire on one side, and the warm, human, emotional, impoverished, culturally inferior (in the eyes of white settlers), ignorant, black population on the other. Or perhaps the paradigm is even more personal: Doris Lessing torn between the remote, aloof father and the emotional, irrational, less admirable mother of the *Children of Violence* novels. The greatest yearning in the *Canopus* series and in earlier books is for unity to occur among the three entities, for a Lock, in the Canopean sense, to bind separateness into benign unity.[6]

Although the colonial's perception of the world informs all Lessing's writing and is merely amplified in the *Canopus* series, other aspects of the space fiction novels are relatively new in the Lessing *oeuvre* and are intimately connected with the aging process. One such aspect is the extremely long and impersonal view of terrestrial doings posited by these books, in which the personal, the social, and the political are reduced to insignificance. That such a perspective is a departure for Lessing is clear from a statement she made while working on the *Children of Violence* series, that she believed the hope of humankind lies in the resting point between the private and the social self,[7] a notion that enlivens and provides tension in much of her early work. The Four-Gated City itself, for example, represents both a collective and a personal ideal, "the ideal state": and the "wholeness of self."[8] The Outsider, caught between the ideal on one side and the "me" on the other is a powerful exemplar of the late twentieth-century human condition in which one cannot ignore the political and social even while hopelessly enmeshed in the personal. This balance shifts in Lessing's fiction. She has written books in which the individual explores the politics of the Left and others in which the subject is the highly personal politics of madness. In the former the ideal is the perfect city; in the latter the perfect individual. The break, however, from this earlier work to *Canopus in Argos*, is more pronounced and reflects movement from youth and growth to age and resignation. In these new books, Lessing investigates the politics of the cosmos, merging the ideal state and the ideal individual into a highly impersonal system in which Ambien can be addressed as

"Sirius," Klorathy as "Canopus," and Al.Ith's lovemaking affects the fertility of her entire zone. In these books, the individual is entirely subsumed into a state so enormous and absolute that it ceases to have any conventional political meaning.

One of Canopus's disturbing aspects for many admirers of Lessing's earlier realist fiction is the elitist hierarchy it postulates, a hierarchy that tends to be dualistic on various levels from the personal to the cosmic: the male mode is superior to the female;[9] immortal is superior to mortal; the Empire is superior to the Colony; the Necessity is superior to the Subversion; Good is superior to Evil. Perhaps this simplification results from the clear-sighted honesty with which Lessing has always regarded the human condition. The form of her earlier works is fairly consistent in presenting, as Jenny Taylor says, an "individual [who] moves through the social world, through proscribed social roles, in the quest for an authentic self, for freedom and knowledge, and, in the process, particularly through the specific position of women, calls the power structure of that world into question — yet without being able to offer any personal or political solution."[10] Possibly the frustration of confronting this unresolvable dilemma in book after unflinching book (and, by extension, in her life) forced Lessing at age sixty to revise her schema in the *Canopus* series: there questing and questioning themselves are seen as willful apostasy from the Necessity which is always transcendently present, would one only align one's stubborn, blind self with it. In this revised perspective, solutions are available, even irresistible, but they are not part of the personal or political arenas which concerned Lessing's pre-Canopus protagonists; instead they are cosmic and absolute.

Lessing terms these cosmic and absolute answers the Necessity, which Ellen Cronan Rose has described as being, like Milton's Providence, "an inscrutable yet benevolent design tending to ultimate and universal harmony."[11] Canopus, the only one of the three intergalactic empires attuned to the Necessity, executes its designs, creating on a universal scale a world strangely reminiscent of the British Empire in its heyday and combating the failings and malice of the other two, erring empires. In the course of reading the *Canopus* series, one gathers that: (1) Canopus colonizes with the benign intention of bringing everyone into alignment with the Necessity; (2) Sirius, unaware of the Necessity, colonizes with benign intention but flawed and exploitative application; and (3) Puttiora, exemplified by its criminal planet, Shammat, colonizes with malign intention to exploit subject peoples. But whatever needs to be learned or changed, imperialism is the universal mode. There is never any question about colonizing itself: it is the How that is examined in Lessing's universe, not the What. Imperialism is the law of the galaxy. The inferiority of subject peoples is assumed and explained in Darwinian terms of greater or lesser evolutionary sophistication. Because these empires are cosmic and the time spans involved are vast, the reader does not immediately question what would seem rank racism and brutality if occurring on earth (or Rohanda, or Shikasta—the renamings of planets are as arbitrary as British renamings of African territories) in a less millennial time scheme. At times, the Canopean Empire resembles nothing so much as a cosmic concentration camp with its directors piously insisting, "It's for your own good and the good of evolving consciousness," as they march various undesirables off to the ovens or to centers for experimentation.

Indeed, in these new books Lessing does not analyze the often painful and exploitative power relations that can exist between and among real people. Instead, the power relations in her new cosmos are an institutionalized, impersonal, acceptable, part of the Necessity. In fact, the Canopean fictions seem to hinge on complicated tortures of colonized peoples for obscure imperialist ends. Whole Shikastan races are exterminated; Al.Ith is made to marry Ben Ata against her will; Ambien becomes a cosmic outcast because of her interest in Canopean ideas; all the inhabitants of Planet 8 undergo ghastly rigors during their interminable Ice Age as a prelude to extinction. And, further, the characters with whom the readers identify—Shikastans especially—are particularly anguished puppets of the master Canopean race. As early as her first novel, *The Grass Is Singing*, which is about the sociology and psychology of apartheid, strongly and simply stated in the intimate context of two individuals, Lessing demonstrated her interest in race relations and imperialism. In the early book, though, black culture is portrayed sympathetically; British imperialist-racist assumptions are seen unsympathetically. But in these late books, Lessing seems to have reversed her opinions. In *Canopus in Argos* the imperialist nation is everything it claims to be, and the subject colonies are as inferior as any committed racist might wish. It is unlikely that Lessing has become a racist,but she may very well be an ageist. That is, the Canopeans have all the virtues associated with age: experience, wisdom, aloofness from emotional hysteria, long-sightedness, resignation to cosmic rhythms. The inferior races have all the volatile complementary "vices" an ageist might associate with youth.

The aging process and Lessing's reaction to it also help explain the shift in the Canopus novels from the human to the galactic. Although Lessing has never been wildly optimistic in her prognosis for the human family, she *has* hinted that struggle may lead to growth and individual and group progress. The *Canopus* series, though, offers only despair for anything as limited as a human being living less than a century. The only hope is cosmic: the Necessity will prevail. Although Lessing's new world view may be distressing to her usual readership, it does encourage a lengthened perspective, which may be characterized as the perspective of old age. In the *Canopus* series there is drawing back, resignation and insistence on a long view.

The pre-*Canopus* books offered a world in which no answers to existential questions were readily available because there were no absolutes, but in which individual struggle had its own nobility and brought its own obscure personal rewards. It was a world in which hierarchies were meaningless because wisdom was as likely—more likely—to come from a young madwoman as an aged seer, and anything as monolithic and complacent as the British Empire was automatically suspect, particularly in its power relations. Above all, it was a world that dignified struggle and looked askance at resignation. Although Lessing's various protagonists were often wrong, crazy, too emotional, paralyzed, immature, obsessed with sex and politically extremist, it was also the case that in these pre-Canopean books, as Susan Kress says, "no novelist convince[d] us more forcefully of the need to change ourselves actively, morally and responsibly."[12]

Now, what are the implications of the shifts in the *Canopus in Argos* series to absolutist answers; resignation, obliteration of the differentiation between the personal and the political; revered hierarchies and acceptance of brutal power relations? In the new books hope has receded into cosmic mists. Our earth is a condemned experiment. Possibilities and opportunities cease. The universe looks toward death, decay, and dissolution, except in a disembodied resurrection in the New Jerusalem, the heaven of the Canopean home planet, about which we are told but which we never see.

We must, perhaps, regard this new series as much more personal than it appears, as, in fact, not cosmic at all, but a map of Doris Lessing's own aging process. It is evident that all Lessing's work is linked to personal experience, even when she is not writing overt autobiography. This premise seems especially tenable when the Canopus books are juxtaposed to the Jane Somers books, *The Diary of a Good Neighbor* and *If the Old Could . . .* , both meditations on the theme of aging, written contemporaneously with the *Canopus* series. Many readers wondered where Lessing's lifelong commitment to realism went when she created Canopus. Jane Somers may provide an answer: she is an underground *doppelgänger* of Doris Lessing. If the Jane Somers books are allowed to comment on the Canopus novels, parallels are apparent. The two series, indeed, resemble Anna Wulf's fragmentation in the notebooks: the political and transcendent inform the Canopus books while the now-despised personal is relegated to pseudonymous Jane Somers. But both series deal with decay, dissolution, and aging. In the Canopean galaxies, planets live and die. In the Jane Somers books, Janna, the author's alter ego, middle-aged, involves her life with women in extreme, often decrepit old age and with young, grasping people on the way up. Both series deal with hierarchical relations between powerful, wise people like Klorathy and Janna and helpless ignorant ones like Maudie; Janna's nieces, Jill and Kate; Ambien; Incent; and

Doeg, a few of whom are capable of growth. The tone in the Jane Somers books and the *Canopus* series is pervasively sad, teasing and grieving. Both series are full of interactions that may reflect the triumphs, the indignities, and the humiliations of aging. Equally, both series are full of powerful characters who, despite their subtle sadism and aloofness, reflect the wisdom and detachment of age. In these late works, Doris Lessing may be—like Tolstoy, whom she so admires, in *Ivan Illych* and some of the other late, great stories—recording the process of aging, of facing the bitterness of mortality, of waning powers, of resignation to forces outside oneself.

There are certainly enormous problems for many readers in dealing with both the *Canopus in Argos* series and the Jane Somers books. Yet both series may presage a new period of creative vitality for Doris Lessing, one in which she will map the little-known and surely frightening territory of old age. Right now the reader may regard the two sets of books as experiments, the blueprints of a great writer and creative genius as she gropes toward new territory, territory scary enough to force the fragmentation familiar from *The Golden Notebook* and *The Four-Gated City*. Now that Jane Somers is out of the closet, perhaps in volume six of *Canopus in Argos: Archives*, or some other future book, she will merge with Klorathy, Johor, Doeg, and the other voices of the Canopean Empire. Doris Lessing may yet give us a fully integrated glimpse of the world of old age in which struggle no longer seems relevant; in which helplessness must be accepted; in which the physical falls away like a badly fitting suit; in which a lifetime seems a minute; in which the necessity for resignation to cosmic order becomes inevitable.

NOTES

1. J. Hillis Miller, *The Form of Victorian Fiction* (Notre Dame, Ind.: University of Notre Dame Press, 1968), 1.

2. Rebecca O'Rourke, "Doris Lessing: Exile and Exception," in *Notebooks/Memoirs/Archives: Reading and Rereading Doris Lessing*, ed. Jenny Taylor (London: Routledge & Kegan Paul, 1982), 221.

3. Doris Lessing, quoted in prologue in *Notebooks/Memoirs/Archives*.

4. Nicole Ward Jouve, "Of Mud and Other Matter—*The Children of Violence*," in *Notebooks/Memoirs/Archives*, 102.

5. Ibid., 102-103.

6. For discussions of this yearning for unity in Lessing's pre-Canopus work, see Carol P. Christ, "From Motherhood to Prophecy: Doris Lessing," *Diving Deep and Surfacing: Women Writers on Spiritual Quest* (Boston: Beacon Press, 1980), 55-73; and Jean Pickering, "Marxism and Madness: The Two Faces of Doris Lessing's Myth," *Modern Fiction Studies* 26 (Spring 1980): 17-30.

7. Doris Lessing, "The Small, Personal Voice," in *Declaration*, ed. Tom Maschler (London: McGibbon & Kee, 1957), 24.

8. Pickering, "Marxism and Madness," 21.

9. See Pickering, "Marxism and Madness," 21; and Marion Vlastos, "Doris Lessing and R.D. Laing: Psychopolitics and Prophecy," *PMLA* 91 (1976): 245-58.

10. Jenny Taylor, "Introduction: Situating Reading," in *Notebooks/Memoirs/Archives*, 5.

11. Ellen Cronan Rose, "Let's Take Doris Lessing's 'Space Fiction' Seriously," (unpublished paper, 1984).

12. Susan Kress, "Lessing's Responsibility," *Salmagundi* 47-48 (Winter-Spring 1980): 131.

Lorna Sage

Lessing and Atopia

Canopus in Argos circles back on *Children of Violence,* not only in its transformations of once-realist themes—relations between cultures and between generations—but also in its engagement with questions of ideological violence and fiction's aspiration to transcend the war of words, or at the least, to postpone that war indefinitely. The "atopia" of my title is a notion borrowed from Roland Barthes. He uses it to locate the text, or suspend it, in the world of language, and it's a useful starting point because it brings into play spatial metaphors:

> We are all caught up in the truth of languages, that is, in their regionality. . . . For each jargon (each fiction) fights for hegemony . . . if power is on its side, it spreads everywhere . . . but even out of power, even when power is against it, the rivalry is reborn, the jargons split and struggle among themselves. A ruthless *topic* rules the life of language; language always comes from some place, it is a warrior *topos*.[1]

Only the text, Barthes suggests, is atopic, plural, paradoxically at peace. Is *Canopus* a text in this sense? Certainly there's a striking coincidence between the atmosphere in which Lessing's space fiction replays her early colonial themes and Barthes's evocation of the curious calm that prevails in the modern text, as—for example—Betsy Draine has pointed out.[2] The "regionality" of language, its coming "always from some place," and the way in which the languages of opposition "split and struggle among themselves"—these were the peculiar agonies of the writing of *Children of Violence*. Early on in *Martha Quest*, for example, we are told that "each group, community, clan, colour, strove and fought away from each other in a sickness of dissolution . . . as if the principle of separateness was bred from the very soil."[3] These are too, recognizably enough, among the problems the *Canopus* series space-shuttled into no-man's-land.

Or to put it quite another (more pleasurable) way, the space fiction seems to take on the guilty colonial drives toward "expansion and development" and take the harm out of them. Lessing the writer has, as she says in the prefatory remarks to *Shikasta* "made—or found—a new world for myself, a realm where the petty fates of planets, let alone individuals, are only aspects of cosmic evolution expressed in the rivalries and interactions of great galactic Empires. . . ."[4] But can her readers share in her exhilaration? Her tone suggests that her "new world" ("made—or found") is empty space for expanding into, but of course it's not. Repetition, indeed, turns out to be one of its main formal and thematic conventions. Here, I'll be picking up on the "colonizing" metaphor, repeated from *Children of Violence*, which provides the framework for all but (perhaps) one of the *Canopus* novels to date. (That one, *The Marriages between Zones Three, Four and Five*, is much the "newest," the most invented, the most obviously pleasurable.) The persistent colonial model provides a focus for considering the newness of Lessing's new world and its possible pluralism. One odd indication that *Canopus* may not have proved plural enough: the recent revelation that from around the time of the third novel, *The Sirian Experiments* in 1981, Lessing was planning and executing a special kind of literary hoax. She wrote and published the two novels that now appear as *The Diaries of Jane Somers*, under the name of Jane Somers. Given her decentering of the narrative voice in *Canopus*, and her attacks on rhetoric that "comes from some place," the invention of Jane Somers is suggestive in several ways. For the moment, I'd like simply to recall that Lessing broke the sequence of *Children of Violence* around the third novel too, with *The Golden Notebook*. "Jane Somers," it seems already safe to say, won't count anything like so much; but there's a hint here of a pattern—a need to break out of one's project—which, again, suggests that the new world has something (something problematic) in common with the old.

"Shedding the Rhetoric of Empire, which they are prepared to analyze with acumen and to reject with scorn and contempt, they become prisoners of the Rhetoric of oppositional groups...."[5] This is the weary voice of Canopus in *The Sentimental Agents in the Volyen Empire*, describing how yet another generation is conned and conscripted by the armies of words. Lessing's impatience to arrive at the end of what's called in *Shikasta* "The Age of Ideology" is explicit, written out, announced. It's there too in the formal insistence that "history" is a function of geography or cosmography and in the "archival" strategies that cut up and juxtapose the narratives. Talk of—say—"the force of history," all the rhetoric of opposition, is bred from the soil in the form of people's atavistic need to belong to the group, to herd together. In *The Sentimental Agents*, Canopus pays ironic homage to the urgency of this need by listing and proliferating names we (they?) have for designating difference: "races, kinds, types, nations, classes, sorts, genders, breeds, strains, tribes, clans, sects, castes, varieties, grades, even species . . ." (p. 161). From the Canopean point of view, difference is, as it were, what all these have in common. Their more fully evolved version of the group mind envisages a whole where differences coexist, and Need with a capital N is studied and understood, and so on. This whole-versus-group theme shapes all the *Canopus* novels and can be seen at work—for instance—in the large-scale irony of *The Sirian Experiments*, where the managerial narrator, Ambien, becomes a "traitor" because she realizes that all along the seemingly rival Empire had included her. Or again, in *The Marriages between Zones Three, Four, and Five*, when the Zone Four women form themselves into what looks very like a women's movement and get imaginatively lost as a result, on an untimely pilgrimage to Zone Three. The group turns out to be a travesty of the whole.

These plots both celebrate heterogeneity and render it permanently provisional. My earlier quotation from *The Sentimental Agents* listing "races, kinds, types, nations," and so forth, ends with the words "all of them united by *waiting*." So difference is, seemingly, depoliticized. Canopeans don't deal in debate; they're unable to explain themselves and pursue a gnostic paradoxical "silent" speech that's meant to undermine rhetoric and make others wait. A quotation from Ambien in *The Sirian Experiments*, describing a Canopean agent on a cultural mission to a primitive people, follows:

> He spoke of places "beyond the waters" where an advanced medicine was used based on local balances and earth forces. . . . They did *not* hear. They *could* not hear. I have never before seen so clearly and simply illustrated that law of development that makes a certain stage of growth impossible to an individual, a people, a planet: first they have to hear?[6]

In context this is crushingly ironic, because it's Ambien herself who's (still) primitive and who's being hard of hearing. Communication between different cultures is delayed, difficult, partial, never complete. Because (to use Barthes again): "A ruthless *topic* rules the life of language; language always comes from some place." Speaking is superseded by listening, waiting, "reading." Dialogue (like Platonic dialogue, like—presumably—Sufi teaching techniques) is about "turning the mind round" so that you see new dimensions—new spaces—in what you already know. In *The Making of the Representative for Planet 8*, the planet 8 people are supplied with microscopes for this purpose, so that they can see themselves as composite, a conglomerate of groups, mostly space.

Unsurprisingly, then, one of the most characteristic structuring devices is a kind of synecdoche. The quotation from Ambien, for instance, spells it out, in expansionist form—"an individual, a people, a planet." Whatever you name, in this grammar, is a version of the part-for-the-whole or the other way about. Some more examples, the first—from *The Sirian Experiments*: "Yet most societies, cultures—empires—can be described by an underlying fact or truth, and this is nearly always physical geographical . . ." (p. 80). And, from *The Making of the Representative for Planet 8*: "Our Empire isn't random, or made by the decisions of self-seeking rulers or by the unplanned developments of our technologies. . . . Our growth, our existence, *what we are* is a unit, a unity, a whole. . . ."[7] This last example, which comes from a Canopean agent, more or less betrays the device by naming it: it's a device for pointing always toward an (unachieved) totality. Hence, in *Shikasta*, its ironizing effect in relation to partial, party politics—"Nearly all political people were incapable of thinking in terms of interaction, of cross-influences, of the various sects and 'parties' forming *together* a whole, wholes . . ." (p. 101). Lessing's Canopeans are guardians of difference (they immerse themselves in local conditions, incarnate themselves as historical individuals) and at the same time are subverters of the politics of difference.

They are also, she has insisted, in *The Sirian Experiments*, mere strategies themselves.

> The reason, we all know, why readers yearn to 'believe' cosmologies and tidy systems of thought is that we live in dreadful and marvelous times where the certainties of yesterday dissolve as we live. But I don't want to be judged as adding to a confusion of embattled certainties. (p. 10)

This takes one back to the atopia of the text [writers, she goes on to remind us, " 'make things up,' that is our trade." (p. 10)] She is, though, being disingenuous. It's not so much a question of whether readers "believe in"—say—reincarnation or angelic visitors but of how the narrative voice represents the reader, how the text lets its readers in, and what it lets them in for. *Canopus* is all about the way different cultures occupy ultimately the same space; built into the texture is the assumption that one language, one group code is always part of another larger one. Lessing has of course been talking about this throughout her writing life and seems to have become conscious of it because she was a Communist and a colonial—that is, a member of an oppositional minority within a dominant minority, neither of which acknowledged the positive meaning of race or gender. As I've argued elsewhere, her sense of herself as writer is shaped by the conviction that writing is about *being representative* (not necessarily representational).[8] Two quotations, far apart in time, follow, the first, from her 1957 essay "The Small Personal Voice": "One is a writer at all because one represents, makes articulate, is continuously and invisibly fed by, numbers of people who are inarticulate, to whom one belongs, to whom one is responsible."[9] The second quotation is from the preface to *The Sirian Experiments* in 1981.

> With billions and billions and billions of us on this planet, we are still prepared to believe that each of us is unique, or that if all the others are mere dots in a swarm, then at least *I* am this self-determined thing, my mind my own. Very odd this. . . . How do we get this notion of ourselves?
>
> It seems to me that ideas must flow through humanity like tides. (p. 11)

The tone has changed a lot, of course, but the underlying need to locate an authorial "I" that is potentially "we" is still there. That she has invented a space fiction format in pursuit of it is a measure, it seems to me, of the intensity of her built-in dread of the regional, the partial—"white" Africa, for short.

The most striking legacy, in *Canopus*, is the structuring assumption that different groups inevitably overlap and interfere with each other, so that—to put it crudely—it's not a matter of oppression *or* coexistence but of "good" colonizers or "bad" colonizers. The Canopeans (the good) are the group of groups, always at work to turn wars of words into silent symbiosis, and so on, agents of a (mostly) invisible Empire. And they are—despite their modest disguises—figures of authority, unmistakably. Residual authority, perhaps, but all the more absolute for that. Consider this exchange from *The Making of the Representative for Planet 8*:

> "Again, one person, one individual is made to represent so many!" And, as I spoke, I felt now familiar pressures, the announcement deep in myself of something I should be understanding.
>
> And that was when I let myself go away into sleep, having taken in what I could for that time. And when I woke Johor was sitting patiently, waiting for me to resume. I had not done much more than register: Here I am!—and add to it the thought: But the 'I' of me is not my own, cannot be, must be a general and shared consciousness—when Johor said. . . . (P. 89)

This specimen of "dialogue" (one of many similar, repeated "exchanges") demonstrates the power of silence. Johor, spokesman of Canopus, uses silence to undercut Doeg's speech and prompt him to a "recognition," a kind of invented memory of "shared consciousness." It demonstrates too the much greater authority of something you seem to arrive at yourself, compared with anything you're told. In short, Canopean silence is an insidious style of antirhetorical rhetoric—more potent than speech because it seems to come from everywhere and nowhere, from within, from the landscapes glimpsed in dreams. And so Planet 8 is colonized, or in Canopus-speak evolves into a multiple monad, a voice that says "we." And "we," fairly clearly here, is an imperial, imperative pronoun—"something I *should* be understanding."

Lessing's Canopeans employ a doublespeak that appropriates the voices of others. This is less a way of renouncing authorial power than of retaining it—by identifying with difference. Their patience and their ubiquity make them, in fact, remarkably pure figures of power, the latest (perhaps the last) inheritors of the tradition *Children of Violence* battled within, according to which (in Nicole Ward Jouve's words, my own are wearing thin) "the world of an individual could be put into correspondence with, *represent*, the world."[10] Lessing, who made her own way into the territory of the *nouveau roman* in *The Golden Notebook*, is exposing equally unerringly, autodidact-fashion, the contradictions that lurk in the space of the *text*. Her scornful rejection of "the Rhetoric of oppositional groups" serves to uncover once again "the Rhetoric of Empire," transposed. Michel Foucault, noting the way the author has refused to die, provides a striking analogy.

> In current usage . . . the notion of writing seems to transpose the empirical characteristics of the author into a transcendental anonymity . . . it keeps alive, in the grey light of neutralization, the interplay of those representations that formed a particular image of the author. . . . There seems to be an important dividing line between those who believe that they can still locate today's discontinuities in the historico-transcendental tradition of the nineteenth century, and those who try to free themselves once and for all from that tradition.[11]

Lessing's *Canopus* series criss-crosses this dividing line.

My argument has been that Lessing's excursion into space has exposed how thoroughly her language "comes from some place." In distancing her narrative voice from the "warring certainties" of what she would see as *local* politics, she has arrived at a bleak picture of cultural imperialism. The celebrations of difference in *Canopus* are undercut and contradicted by a totalizing urge, which becomes more—not less—insistent by virtue of the postponement of total order. And this, I think, is what's most interesting about her space fiction; although it seems paradoxical to say so, because it's also what accounts for the large tracts of greyness and the sensation of *deja vu*. One is tempted to try to locate these books in atopia because their combination of continuous local uncertainty and bland authority is anomalous and embarrassing. But they're more provocative and alive as anomalies. They remind us that dialogue is seldom conducted between equals and that the writer in certain crucial senses "speaks for" and represents the reader. The reader (*this* reader, at any rate) often feels dismissed, excluded—or, because I'm using the term, colonized—by a benevolent (and therefore even more exasperating) authority.

Her new world is *not* different, in this sense, not *different* at all. Heterogeneous elements aren't for her contiguous or merely coexistent, but they are always rearranging themselves into parts and wholes. Thinking back to her African stories, and to *Children of Violence*, one can detect the persistence of a thoroughly political, if unmanageable, perception: that the adventure of discovery is always a matter of moving into space *already* inhabited by other kinds, other species, other codes—which in its turn means that power struggles aren't transcended but transposed. The *Canopus* books, with their repetitious plots, their deployment of synecdoche, and their use of silence as the voice of authority, only *look like* texts. Lessing hasn't emigrated to atopia. Witness "Jane Somers"—a mundane voice invented out of the strain (surely) of maintaining the long wait, the interminable delay of *Canopus*. The Jane Somers books are, among other things, "boulder-pushing" novels in the spirit of the end of *The Golden Notebook*: novels about personal responsibility in particular relationships. They are also (to keep the contradictions alive) another manifestation of Lessing's desire to disperse her authorial authority—as if it wasn't dispersed enough as, I've argued, it isn't—*Canopus* is about claustrophobia in space. The problem of decentering the author seems for Lessing so far insoluble (although the Somers hoax was a witty comment on it). Luckily insoluble, perhaps? Instead of saying that these novels only "look like" texts, one might suggest that they reveal something that's true of many "texts"—that they *do* take up space, not only on bookshelves and that the question of who represents whom, who speaks for "us," is still a political question.

NOTES

1. Roland Barthes, *The Pleasure of the Text*, trans. Richard Miller (New York: Farrar, Straus & Giroux, 1975), 28.

2. Betsy Draine, *Substance under Pressure: Artistic Coherence and Evolving Form in the Novels of Doris Lessing* (Madison: University of Wisconsin Press, 1983), 28.

3. Doris Lessing, *Martha Quest* (St. Albans, England: Panther, 1966), 56.

4. Doris Lessing, *Shikasta* (St. Albans, England: Panther, 1981), 8. All references are to this edition; subsequent references appear in parentheses in the text.

5. Doris Lessing, *The Sentimental Agents in the Volyen Empire* (London: Cape, 1983), 29. All references are to this edition; subsequent references appear in parentheses in the text.

6. Doris Lessing, *The Sirian Experiments* (St. Albans, England: Panther, 1982), 263. All references are to this edition; subsequent references appear in parentheses in the text.

7. Doris Lessing, *The Making of the Representative for Planet 8* (St. Albans, England: Panther, 1983), 80. All references are to this edition; subsequent references appear in parentheses in the text.

8. Lorna Sage, *Doris Lessing*, (London & New York:Methuen, 1983), 46.

9. Doris Lessing, "The Small Personal Voice" in *A Small Personal Voice*, ed. Paul Schuleter (New York: Vintage, 1975), 20-21.

10. Nicole Ward Jouve, "Of Mud and Other Matter—*The Children of Violence*," in *Notebooks/Memoirs/Archives: Reading and Rereading Doris Lessing*, ed. Jenny Taylor (London: Routledge & Kegan Paul, 1982), 75-134, 126.

11. Michel Foucault, "What is an Author?" in *Textual Strategies*, ed. J.V. Harari (London: Methuen, 1979), 141-60, 144-45.

Eve Bertelsen

Who is it who says "I"?: The Persona of a Doris Lessing Interview

In an interview with a Great Author I look for and find the transcendental signified: the unique obsessions of the historical author, Doris Lessing, the originating source, presence, voice, which has spoken an *oeuvre* of texts sanctified to Literature by admiring readers and the critical industry. Here there can be no masking: the enunciative authorial figure is palpably present. I confront a superfluity of Jakobsonian shifters. The real author finally says "I." I have tracked down *the* primary source.

Or have I? This, at least, seems to be the received position on the literary interview, one which is seldom thrown in question. What I begin to do in this short paper is to problematize the interview as discourse and as a practice with political implications. I contend that, far from giving us a moment of unproblematic presence, an interview forms, rather, one moment in a complex and ongoing struggle, a contest for control of the ways in which reality is to be signified, and within that field, the ways in which Lessing's texts in particular may be consumed. Concentrating on my own interview with Lessing[1] I trace some of the marks of such a struggle. I place it in a cycle of production, distribution, and consumption. I suggest that rather than an originating and spontaneous voice, what we have to do with is a text which is in a profound sense already written, a space already occupied: occupied in the sense that its forms, procedures, and even its eventual consumption have already been fixed by a host of received assumptions about what constitutes an interview and about the status and authority of its primary speaker. And criticism has also predetermined how such a text will be consumed and the uses to which it will be put in teaching and research.

Here I focus on the productive phase. I look at Lessing's strenuous intervention: her insistence on retaining control of the meaning of her texts in opposition to the troublesome scenario of an interviewer who seeks to discover some of the historical, literary, and political determinants of her writing practices. The battle that ensues is interesting, although I hope to show that the knowledge thus produced is highly problematical.

The interview's persona appears to be constructed in distinct stages as the text passes from oral conversation and verbatim transcript to its final edited version (in the case of my interview, two and a half hours and 100 pages to a 20-page edited text). I suggest that conventional editing procedures are ideological, because they serve to reinforce the expressive illusion, eliminate uncertainty and contradiction, and standardize authorial dicta to the body of extant commentary, offering up a cohesive, closed, and serviceable text.

This paper suggests how we might begin to open up the authorial voice as something authoritative and already finished and discover the terms of the discourse: some of those distinctive modes of operation which are "Lessing." In place of the usual public relations role adopted by criticism (placing texts, fixing their meanings, reproducing the positions of their author, and in every way smoothing the passage between the texts and their readers), I propose one strategy for occupying them in a different way.

THE INTERVIEWS

MICHEL FOUCAULT POINTS TO THE POWERFUL FUNCTION of the author's name on a text: it designates a definite historical figure in which a series of events converge; it defines a level of quality, a conceptual coherence, and a stylistic uniformity.[2]

I have said that as critics we use Lessing's pronouncements in her interviews (and Prefaces too) to verify and legitimate assessments of her work. We use them as proof of her intentions, her evolving frame of values, her experience, her place within literary systems, and her characteristic mind-style. In epigraphs, at crucial points in arguments and in conclusions, quotations from interviews serve to clinch an interpretation, to fix, as it were, the signifiers to the transcendental signified and produce a definitive reading. They serve also to establish an *oeuvre* of texts out of which is constructed that mainstay of criticism, the notional author—those continuities of theme and style that constitute another text, a metatext or language, which is then read back into the single text, determining our expectations and recognitions. In this way, a convenient and self-validating system of cross-reference is established within which the interview plays its part, as the historical author, the originating presence or voice, confirms, delimits, and fixes forever the text's meaning and the procedures of reading.

Foucault introduces into this cycle some new questions: "What are the modes of existence of this discourse? Where does it come from; how is it circulated; who controls it? What placements are determined for possible subjects?"

I have not the space here to engage with the wider field of circulation and control (publishing, media, marketing, readership), but I will outline in the single instance of my recent interview with Lessing what I perceive to be the signs of a discourse of authorial control.

THE CONVERSATION/TRANSCRIPT

IN ITS ORAL PHASE, THE INTERVIEW IS A CONVERSAtion, a dialogue between a primary and a secondary speaker. Here, the primary speaker is Lessing, the author who has produced an *oeuvre* of texts. She owns these texts in a material sense via copyright and royalty agreements and has a limited say in their distribution. Her real power as an author, however, derives from the frames of knowledge encoded into the texts which offer specific subject positions for their readers and determine their preferred reading or interpretation. Once the texts are freely distributed, how is she to retain ideological control? One way is by offering interviews in which she develops an authorial metacommentary which will reinforce and fix the disposition of her work.

The secondary speaker in this case is the critic/interviewer (EB). I am a consumer of the *oeuvre*, but a consumer of a special kind. I am part of the network of distribution and appropriation in which the prescribing of Lessing texts in the syllabi of higher education and a supportive body of commentary legitimates the texts as "higher culture" and endorses their evaluations. My knowledge of both the texts themselves and of this scholarly commentary equips me with a *critical* overview to match the *authorial* metaview. I come equipped also with my own hypothesis concerning the trajectory of her life's work, her evolving style, and its links with her changing political positions. Finally, I have scrutinized twenty previous interviews for silences, repetitions, and discursive strategies. I am determined to fill the lacunae. As a native South African I am unlikely to be seduced by the customary set pieces ("Africa, that old wound, that ache in the blood . . ."). She is going to answer those questions previous interviewers either have not asked or she has declined to answer. I know that she dislikes critics, and university teachers in particular. These are the dynamics of the situation. As Great Author she is in a strong position. As a perceptive woman she stereotypes me from the start: South African, radical, intellectual, critic. She is determined to control the discussion. Although I appear to be calling the shots, I must be cautious (she has been known to throw people out); I must downgrade my own contributions (in all modesty, nobody is waiting for my words). She is an old hand at this game. It is my first interview. She sits obligingly on a pouf at my feet. I switch on the tape. We begin.

What ensues is something like a battle, which loses all of its most interesting and dramatic features in the process of editing and transition to print, the final version offering a bland précis of what actually occurs. To put it briefly, the mode of discourse represented by an oral interview is dramatic, specific, concrete, ephemeral, subject to idiosyncratic ruptures with prose syntax, repetitive, often contradictory, iconic as well as verbal, simultaneous rather than linear, as we speak over one another, nod, smile, frown, contradict, struggle for ascendancy, feel each other out.

My limited task here is to try to define the "persona" of the interview, and I suggested that this is to be found in the "mode of existence" of the discourse, its mode of operation, which I have defined as a mode of fixing and control. In order to ground such a claim in the language itself, I will use some broad headings of conversation analysis[3] and comprehensive discourse analysis.[4] I point to Lessing's refusal of my line of questioning and my partial recovery by way of a series of rephrasals to elicit at least some answers. Finally, I identify the agendas which I see as overdetermining the power struggle represented by the exchange and make some comments on the practices of editing. My aim in all this is to problematize the interview as language/control and to throw into question the use of interviews as a simple and expressive source of truth. I must emphasize that this method deliberately avoids treating of the text as "content," focusing rather on its "disposition" as discourse. (The appendix contains typical passages, referred to below passim.)

TOPIC SELECTION AND MANIPULATION OF VERBAL CUES

TO AVOID REPETITION OF PREVIOUS INTERVIEWS, I zone in on the gaps. My broad theme is Africa, and under this heading I want to discuss her literary and political development from the 1940s to the present. She initially refuses each topic itself and my phrasing of the questions. I talk about settler myths: DL—"I don't see the veld as a myth but a fact"; realism in "The Small Personal Voice": DL—"Well, I think I was talking nonsense;" (A, in the appendix); style: DL—"Style is not something abstract, it's a way of thinking, it's feeling"; the influence of Schreiner: DL—"No, not at all"; Gordimer: DL—"You know you've got the play thing on there"; D.H. Lawrence: DL—"It astounds me that it's reminiscent of *Lady Chatterley's Lover*!"

The words "style," "politics," and "development" are invariably treated as negative cues (for example, B in the appendix). I remind her that she was an editor of the Communist *New Reasoner*: DL—"No, I wasn't!" (she was), followed by "It's no use asking me about the British Communist Party" (I hadn't). When pressed about her political development, she mounts a preemptive strike by caricaturing the critics (and by implication, the interviewer): DL—"That's how their minds work, you see. But each time it's labels they haven't examined" (She will brook no examination now). Throughout the exchange she she was a mystic and now she's a Sufi.' That's how it goes, you see. But each time it's labels they haven't examined." (She will brook no examination now.) Throughout the exchange she changes topics at will, introducing autobiographical vignettes in response to conceptual questions, or generalizing when asked for a detail. For example, she attacks me at regular intervals for being "abstract" and invariably follows this up with the broadest generalizations herself (see B in the appendix: Lessing admits to utilizing the "quest" myth then refuses to acknowledge it as a binding structure in the novels).

The standard explanations for "discourse failure" can, I think, readily be ruled out. This is no mere matter of misunderstanding or confusion but a tenacious manipulation of the terms of the discourse, both in choice of topics and of the actual words and categories employed. Nor is the whole as perfunctory as these examples imply. She is generous with information, often speaking for many minutes on end, but seldom in response to my plan or specific questions, always according to a logic and in a language which she will define.

Metatalk

An important mode of control is Lessing's caricaturing of critics (myself in particular) which is established in an ongoing and confrontational foregrounding of her questioner's language. This strategy serves to displace the topic in hand and assert control. These remarks are often prefaced by phrases such as "You're talking as if . . ." or "You all talk as if . . ." A few typical examples are:

"You're talking very abstractly, I don't know if you know that."

"Not at all! Why do you people always try to make links where no links exist? It's an academic game you play!"

"I've been steadily appalled at the level of criticism...the standard gets lower and lower . . . it isn't a help to literature, it's the opposite." "What on earth has this kind of argument or discussion . . . what interest is it to anyone except people who are going to teach literature in universities? None whatsoever! To people who actually read books, finding some use for them . . . it's quite irrelevant!" (see A in the appendix for original phrasing). "They all pursue their own lines...which has got nothing to do with writing." "What you want me to do is write didactic novels!" (God forbid!) "All the time you're talking as if the writer imposes an idea on the material instead of writing from inside" (see B in the appendix).

These comments culminate in a magnificent set piece toward the end of the interview in which Lessing pronounces a radical catechism, which she maintains she is being expected to sign.

> I mean, this is really what they want. . . . This is what people want. I can write fifty books with all kinds of different attitudes in them, but it's not enough, you see.

What I have to do is, there should be twenty-one points that "I believe in"—the equality of the races and so forth. And sign it, and then everyone would be pleased. I find this very primitive!

MANIPULATION OF NONVERBAL CUES

AT CRUCIAL POINTS IN THE INTERVIEW THE TAPE recorder, cats, horses passing by in the road, and so forth, serve to completely derail an unwanted line of questioning. This aspect of the discourse only becomes apparent in a study of the transcript. In each case I forget what was at issue and move on to a new topic. Facial and vocal cues of amusement, disagreement, interest, and concern are also skillfully assessed and put to strategic use, and Lessing's own body language, tone of voice, and facial expressions are commandingly deployed for emphasis (see A in the appendix).

TURNTAKING AND REFUSALS

CONVERSATION ANALYSTS TALK OF "ADJACENCY PAIRS."[5] Exchanges are divided into two parts: in each the first unit anticipates a preferred second part. For example:

A: Will you pass me the salt?

B: Yes, sure (preferred) (dispreferred: No!)

A striking feature of Lessing's responses in my interview is that she persistently offers the *dispreferred* response. Examples abound. Often they are complex, involving a rephrasing of terms, metatalk, or a combination of the displacements I have outlined above. But on at least eight occasions she gives a blunt "No" to questions simply asking for confirmation of statements she has made elsewhere. For example:

EB: "Did you identify with Lyndall?" DL: No, not at all!"

EB: "Doesn't Martha's city in the veld symbolize a classless society?"

DL: "No, it doesn't."

EB: "Did that come from your political attitudes at the time?"

DL: "No, it was the other way round. . . ."

EB: "In *Landlocked* the rain has this mythological overtone. . . ."

DL: "By the way, has it rained in South Africa yet? In the Matabeleland area?" (See also the whole pattern of exchanges in A, B, and D in the appendix.)

There is considerable overlap between the categories I am using, so that Lessing's refusals would also include all the strategies discussed above. A close analysis of her persistent violation of the rules of turntaking would probably involve a scrutiny of her syntax, which often functions to swivel the question around, so that she may redefine it and answer it on her own terms. Some regular markers are: "No . . . , but I suppose you could say," "Not at all, what I really meant was . . . ," and "What you are really trying to say is. . . ." (I was not.) (See A, B, and D in the Appendix.)

Repair Mechanisms

It is important to say that the combative tenor of the discussion was by no means unrelated to my own tenacity of purpose. I have already briefly characterized my own motivations under Conversation, above. A longer study would obviously need to deconstruct the discourses of both primary *and* secondary speakers. Here a brief comment must suffice. In the original interview, my role is obviously and intentionally intrusive. In insisting on filling the gaps in previous interviews I am, for my own part, refusing Lessing's own conscious and unconscious choices: her suppressions, her rewriting of her past, and her preferred reading of her work. It seems clear to me now that a good deal of Lessing's resistance to my line of questioning also has to do with a rather uncanny equivalence between my present position (South African, radical, historical materialist) and that of her own rejected past, and that I was probably driven to make this present "analysis after the event" by a desire to understand this tension more clearly. I registered this tension at the time at an intuitive level, as a pervasive sense of mutual mistrust, shot through, it must be added, with moments of shared humor and nostalgia. It seems to me that these elements in no way detract from my argument. I would submit that it is precisely my refusal or disruption of Lessing's "sealing" metacommentary on her life and work that serves to foreground so clearly and thus offer up for analysis the strategies of such a discourse. At any rate, my immediate task was to stay in there and elicit answers. To this end I found it necessary to resort to a number of "repair mechanisms" which serve to lower the level of conflict and allow the questioning to proceed again on a more even keel. We spend long stretches of precious tape time chatting about our respective African childhoods, the drought in Matabeleland, my missionary parents, and various friends and enemies of Lessing's I have met. It is interesting that these are the only parts of the conversation punctuated with rapturous "Yes!"'s and phrases of confirmation and agreement. Other repair initiators on my part are cued by phrases like:

"No, I don't, really!" "I was just . . ." "But at the time you did say . . . ,"

"But you were . . . ," "It's just that . . . ," "What I really meant was . . . ,"

"I may sound abstract, but . . . ," "So you don't think that . . . ," and so forth.

In these cases the onus of apology or rephrasing is placed on the questioner if the dialogue is not to break down completely. In this way I am able to backtrack on several questions that have previously been refused, and by rephrasing them, finally elicit answers. A typical example would be:

EB: "So you are much more aware of the styles you are employing than the critics allow?"

DL: "Yes, well of course they're not very bright, you know!"—followed by a detailed comment on voices, register, satire, allegory, symbolism in a number of her novels. (See also A and D in the appendix.)

SET PIECES

THE MOST SEDUCTIVE STRETCHES OF THE INTERVIEW, and so, for the purposes of this analysis at least, the least instructive, are Lessing's series of beautifully fashioned vignettes. Some of these have occurred before (childhood on the veld; talk on Rhodesian verandas; criticism of feminism and the peace movement), but several are new. These passages are of course retained in full in the printed version (see Final Edit, below). What interests me here is that such pieces seldom appear in response to any specific question, but, as it were, spontaneously, as autonomous and fully formed narratives, more like pieces from any of her journalism or fiction, than elements in an oral discourse or conversation. As such, they fall again under the heading of displacements—none the less valuable and entertaining, of course, for that!

CONTROL

I HAVE FOREGROUNDED SOME OF THE FEATURES OF Lessing's oral discourse and suggested that they constitute a code of authorial control. In doing this I have deliberately resisted referring to the "content" of the interview (those authorial assessments which are traditionally lifted out and deployed as "evidence"). I have concentrated on what may be called its *disposition*. Here, I offer a few general remarks on the patterns I have identified. Lessing's conversation here seems to reveal a comprehensive refusal of the critical enterprise. She rejects all labels and categories as applied to her work. She proposes a holistic and, one might say, simultaneous view of her *oeuvre*, resisting any periodization, development, or calculation. She defends a highly expressive notion of authorship in which her own feelings and experience are communicated directly to her readers, a process in which any mediation by a third party is construed as deliberate subversion. She mischievously derails anything that might begin to resemble a critical debate, insisting on a fluidity whose only logic is pure authorial power. She will define the terms and delimit the range of meanings that may be ascribed to her texts. In short, Lessing fixes the signifiers firmly to the transcendental signified of her own wisdom and experience.

FINAL EDIT AND DISTRIBUTION/CONSUMPTION

AND SO TO THE FINAL PRINTED INTERVIEW WHICH enters the discourse of authorial metacommentary and is grist to the mill of the critical industry. I found that in the process of transcribing a two-and-a-half hour tape and reducing nearly 100 pages of discussion to the marketable maximum of 20 pages, traditional editing practice worked to eliminate almost all traces of the original confrontational discourse. The written codes that are *de rigueur* for academic publication promote consistency, clarity, systematized syntax, a single tone of voice, and the phasing out of the secondary speaker (interviewer). Thus the dicta of the Great Author are consolidated into serviceable wedges of print punctuated only by a series of brief and respectful questions.

If, following Louis Althusser,[6] it is the function of ideology to smooth over ruptures, to resolve contradictions, to conceal the marks of enunciation (the authorial code), and to offer up a naturalized, unitary voice, then the editing of an interview performs this task admirably. And, within this scheme, it makes a lot of sense for the interview to take its place as a primary source in legitimating the "truth value" of the *oeuvre*.

In conclusion, I would submit that if the persona of a Lessing interview can be defined at all, it will have to be something quite different from the common notion of an originating and unproblematic presence. Rather, it appears to be the product of a collaborative enterprise in which writer, interviewer, and critic conspire to retain control over texts and the ways in which they will signify. In the case of Lessing studies, the dominant orthodoxy still tends to be American, and, within that, beset by the contradictions of the New Criticism. This means that while on the one hand texts are deemed to be "autonomous," offering the reader some kernel of self-evident "truth," on the other, the reader is always being carefully aligned by means of the author's own statements of intention and an ever-growing body of normative commentary, to take a limited "preferred" reading of the texts and the *ouevre.* In the process, Lessing's texts are doubly "sealed," reified, and packaged for easy assimilation. By filling the gaps in and between texts and smoothing over their discontinuities, this criticism manages to produce one relatively coherent "Lessing" discourse, an evolving organic continuity of form and meaning. In concert with the author, this commentary *rewrites* or *repeats* the texts, but more harmoniously, concealing their ruptures to deliver their "truth." What I suggest here is that an interesting and instructive aspect of any Lessing text is precisely its *multiplicity* and *incompleteness*, the conflict between its many and changing meanings. To my mind, a radical criticism will work to recognize and differentiate these competing meanings. It asserts that an author's desire to resolve such tensions is the primary artistic impulse and the true reason for the text's composition. Rather than simply work to reinforce this *apparent completeness*, we may position ourselves to begin to explore the unifying strategies themselves and thus begin to grasp the text's *raison d'être*. In doing this, we challenge the orthodoxy which seeks to own and control the *oeuvre* by constructing a single meaning for it. Although this control may be illusory, what it does reflect is an awareness that texts exist from the outset as grounds to be competed for. Here, I suggest one way in which we might create a new subject position for ourselves as critics and occupy in a new and challenging way an apparently simple and unproblematic text.

Notes

1. Eve Bertelsen, "An Interview with Doris Lessing," *Journal of Commonwealth Literature*, 21, no. 2 (1986), and Eve Bertelsen, ed., *Doris Lessing* (Johannesburg: McGraw-Hill, 1986). A short extract is also published in the *Doris Lessing Newsletter*, 9, no. 2 (Fall 1985). Full transcript and tapes available from University of Cape Town.

2. Michel Foucault, "What is an Author?" in *Language, Counter-Memory, Practice* (Oxford: Basil Blackwell, 1977). See also Roland Barthes, "The Death of the Author," in *Image-Music-Text* (London: Fontana, 1977).

3. Stephen C. Levinson, *Pragmatics* (Cambridge: Cambridge Univ. Press, 1983), Chap. 6.

4. William Labov and David Fanshel, *Therapeutice Discourse Analysis* (London: Routledge & Kegan Paul, 1981), esp. Deidre Burton, "Analyzing Spoken Discourse." My headings are freely adapted from this work. Special acknowledgement is due to my colleague Sally Swartz of the Department of Psychology, University of Cape Town, for her guidance.

5. See Levinson.

6. Louis Althusser, "Ideology and Ideological State Apparatuses," in *Lenin and Philosophy and Other Essays* (London: New Left Books, 1981). See also Tony Bennett, *Formalism and Materialism: Developments in Semiology and the Theory of the Subject*, (London: Routledge & Kegan Paul, 1977), esp. Chap. 5, "Marxism, Language, and Ideology."

APPENDIX

INTERVIEWS WITH DORIS LESSING

This is not a complete listing, but it includes most of the substantial interviews up to 1985.

Bannon, B.A. "Authors and Editors." *Publisher's Weekly*, London (2 June 1969).

Bertelsen, Eve. "An Interview with Doris Lessing." *Journal of Commonwealth Literature*, Leeds, 21, no. 2 (1986).

Bergonzi, Bernard. "In Pursuit of Doris Lessing." *New York Review of Books*, New York (11 February 1965).

Bigsby, C.W.E. "Doris Lessing: An Interview." *The Radical Imagination and the Liberal Tradition*, Junction Press, London (1981).

Bikman, Minda. "A Talk with Doris Lessing." *New York Review of Books*, New York (30 March 1980).

Braudeau, Michel. "Doris Lessing: Du Marxisme au Soufisme." *L'Express*, Paris (5 May 1981).

Driver, C.J. "Profile 8: Doris Lessing." *New Review*, London, 1, no. 8 (November 1974).

Hazelton, Lesley. "Doris Lessing on Feminism, Communism and Space Fiction." *New York Times Magazine*, New York (25 July 1982).

Howe, Florence. "A Talk with Doris Lessing." in Paul Schlueter (ed.), *A Small Personal Voice*, Vintage Books, New York (1975).

Langley, L. "Scenarios of Hell." *Guardian Weekly*, London (24 April 1971).

Newquist, Roy. "Interview with Doris Lessing." in Schlueter, *op. cit.* (1975).

Oates, Joyce Carol. "A Visit with Doris Lessing." *Southern Review*, Louisiana, 9, no. 4 (Autumn 1973).

Raskin, Jonah. "Doris Lessing at Stony Brook: An Interview." in Schlueter, *op. cit.* (1975).

Rihiot, Catherine. "Doris Lessing: An Interview." *F. Magazine*, Paris (June 1981).

Thorpe, Michael. "Doris Lessing: Interview." *Kunapipi* (Aarhus, Denmark) 4, no. 2 (1982).

Torrents, Nissa. "Doris Lessing: Testament to Mysticism." translated by Paul Schlueter. *Doris Lessing Newsletter* 4, no. 2 (Winter 1980). Interview was reprinted from *La Calle* (Madrid).

BERTELSEN: INTERVIEW WITH DORIS LESSING.

Some short extracts from full (unedited) transcript.

(A)

But you see I—when critics say this kind of thing my attitude as a writer is, well, they're going to say *something*. I mean they have—let's say—forgive me but there are vast numbers of critics in the world and they have to justify—this is my attitude towards critics—it is of no use to writers and of not much use to readers—it may be of use to other critics—but what—what on earth has got this kind of argument or discussion—what interest is it to anyone except people who are going to teach literature in universities? None whatsoever! To the people who actually read books and enjoy them finding use for—or whatever—it is—it is quite irrelevant. It has got nothing to do with me or with—.

Can I ask you—at a certain stage in your life in—I think in the fifties—you did enter into a polemic where you actually advanced realism and—

Well, I think I was talking nonsense.

Oh, well, that's interesting—because—you know—I tend to have got quite a lot of my enthusiasm for realism from, say, "The Small Personal Voice."

Well, some of the things I said in that were true and some were not. But you know, why should anyone take any notice of an essay written—how many years ago was it—twenty years? I'd—be bound to have changed my mind, wouldn't I?

But at that time you did feel that you were describing what you were trying to do?

Yes. I felt strongly that certain kinds of writing—what was the word I—I felt that they were *ungenerous* I think—that's probably the most accurate word. That they didn't—

You were responding to the "angry young men"—

No I wasn't—. Well—let's talk about the "angry young men"—this illustrates many interesting things about—this—you know that this phenomenon was the total invention of the newspapers. You smile, but it's true.

(B)

Thinking about the Quest story—you know, you choose the name "Quest" for Martha.

I did that on purpose—I wanted to put a name to some part of the character.

And I was wondering, you know, whether as the series continued you became more conscious of creating continuity by reinforcing that quest myth—as she moves through the various phases of her life?

Do you mind my saying that all the time you're talking as if the writer *imposes an idea* on the material instead of writing from *inside*!

VIGNETTE

(C)

Well, you see they talk from morning to night. They get up grumbling and they go to bed grumbling. I've never—it's quite appalling—about everything—everything. I mean a lot of things go wrong—I don't have to tell you—they do—but they have no—they make everything worse, and they *create* problems—I'll describe a little scene which you might not—you won't find surprising. In Umtali, Mutari, in the bank—I wanted to cash checks. And I arrived there just before the doors opened and already a queue of about four whites who stood there bitching—about the incompetence of the blacks. For—they just stood there with these *angry bitter* faces—you know—you look at—you think "for God's sake you're going to *kill* yourselves with hatred if you don't stop it!" Which they *are* of course one way and another. So then, the doors do not open at the stroke of nine because—or half past eight I think it was—because if they could see the man who was—he was looking at these faces and he was thinking "I'll just let them stew"—he was thinking—"these hate filled faces!" Finally the doors open, and then we sit in a line. And the man who we had—there was only one person on—who was changing—there should have been more, true. He was—happened to be a very correctly dressed, very *proper* man—there he was dealing with everyone with this cold, hard correctness and they were standing there with this—these nagging voices—you know these nagging voices—nag, nag, nag, nag, nag—Then finally when I get to him he looked at my passport with his face—he changed—he recognized me. He said "Ah"—he said—"I've read your books!" Can you imagine!—A bank teller—I was so *flattered*! So you see, you get him to chat. And this person is transformed to the most charming, funny, witty—I don't have to tell you—the queue is absolutely *enraged*! And I go out and I think, "If these people were not as stupid as they are, they could be living in a landscape full of charming, witty, and intelligent people." Instead of which they deal all the time with these furious, cold—.

(D)

We've spoken about the Group in Rhodesia. And I think you've said already that it was a fairly Utopian, rather unrealistic experience. But could we talk more about London—and London in the fifties? Because I gather you were on the first editorial board of the Universities and Left Review and the New Reasoner—

No, I wasn't!

Weren't you?

No, I was never on the editorial board. Or if I was, I was just a name on a letterhead. I certainly wasn't involved in the *New Left Review*.

Oh.

Or if I was, I probably said "Well, you can use my name and that's the end of it."

Oh, I see—I think your name was on the first issues.

Oh well—then my name was on it.

But I just wonder if you could reminisce about that? People like John Berger and E.P. Thompson were involved in those magazines weren't they? Did you ever know them?

Ya—I did—I don't think John Berger was involved. E.P. Thompson and John Saville ran the *New Reasoner*.

That's right—John Saville.

And they had one or two meetings at my flat in London. But I wasn't—they ran it—you know—they did it—I never did any of the work. I wrote a short story for them. They were—were and are—I think John Saville—very political. As you know, Edward Thompson has become—what he's doing now—(The Peace Movement) and there were other people around. But you see I was never very much involved in the politics. They were both strong—Edward Thompson and John Saville were Communist party members—working very hard as Communists. And was I—I never was you see. I was—at one point I was a Communist, but I never went to any meetings that—which is a—. It's no good asking me about the British Communist Party. I know quite a bit about the upper echelons of it. The—the grass roots Communist movement I was never part of. I know quite a lot—I knew quite a lot of the fairly well-known names in it. But—I can't talk, for example, about what went on in a Communist party factory group or anything like that.